ST. MAR
ST. MAR

W9-AEJ-355

The Polish Crisis

The Polish Crisis: American Policy Options

A Staff Paper by Jerry F. Hough

THE BROOKINGS INSTITUTION
Washington, D.C.

Copyright © 1982 by
The Brookings Institution
1775 Massachusetts Avenue, N.W., Washington, D.C. 20036

ISBN 0-8157-3743-2
Library of Congress Catalog Card Number 82-072742

1 2 3 4 5 6 7 8 9

Board of Trustees

Robert V. Roosa
Chairman

Andrew Heiskell
Vice Chairman;
Chairman, Executive Committee

Louis W. Cabot
Vice Chairman

Vincent M. Barnett, Jr.
Barton M. Biggs
Frank T. Cary
A. W. Clausen
William T. Coleman, Jr.
Lloyd N. Cutler
Bruce B. Dayton
George M. Elsey
Hanna H. Gray
Huntington Harris
Roger W. Heyns
Bruce K. MacLaury
Robert S. McNamara
Arjay Miller
Herbert P. Patterson
Donald S. Perkins
J. Woodward Redmond
Charles W. Robinson
James D. Robinson III
Henry B. Schacht
Roger D. Semerad
Gerard C. Smith
Phyllis A. Wallace

Honorary Trustees

Eugene R. Black
Robert D. Calkins
Edward W. Carter
Douglas Dillon
John E. Lockwood
William McC. Martin, Jr.
H. Chapman Rose
Robert Brookings Smith
Sydney Stein, Jr.

THE BROOKINGS INSTITUTION is an independent organization devoted to nonpartisan research, education, and publication in economics, government, foreign policy, and the social sciences generally. Its principal purposes are to aid in the development of sound public policies and to promote public understanding of issues of national importance.

The Institution was founded on December 8, 1927, to merge the activities of the Institute for Government Research, founded in 1916, the Institute of Economics, founded in 1922, and the Robert Brookings Graduate School of Economics and Government, founded in 1924.

The Board of Trustees is responsible for the general administration of the Institution, while the immediate direction of the policies, program, and staff is vested in the President, assisted by an advisory committee of the officers and staff. The by-laws of the Institution state: "It is the function of the Trustees to make possible the conduct of scientific research, and publication, under the most favorable conditions, and to safeguard the independence of the research staff in the pursuit of their studies and in the publication of the results of such studies. It is not a part of their function to determine, control, or influence the conduct of particular investigations or the conclusions reached."

The President bears final responsibility for the decision to publish a manuscript as a Brookings book. In reaching his judgment on the competence, accuracy, and objectivity of each study, the President is advised by the director of the appropriate research program and weighs the views of a panel of expert outside readers who report to him in confidence on the quality of the work. Publication of a work signifies that it is deemed a competent treatment worthy of public consideration but does not imply endorsement of conclusions or recommendations.

The Institution maintains its position of neutrality on issues of public policy in order to safeguard the intellectual freedom of the staff. Hence interpretations or conclusions in Brookings publications should be understood to be solely those of the authors and should not be attributed to the Institution, to its trustees, officers, or other staff members, or to the organizations that support its research.

Foreword

FOR MORE than five years the situation in Poland has presented a challenge to U.S. foreign policy. In the late 1970s the problem was how to prevent Poland's burgeoning debt from leading to political collapse—and how to do so when the major instrument available, new credits, would only worsen Poland's debt burden. From September 1, 1980, through December 13, 1981, the problem was how to encourage the survival of Solidarity without taking actions that might provoke the Soviet Union to invade. And since the imposition of martial law, the United States has faced the dilemma of how to put effective pressure on the Polish military regime without harming the Polish people.

In this study, Jerry F. Hough, professor of political and policy sciences at Duke University and an associated staff member of the Brookings Institution, examines the development of the crisis in Poland, the political and economic situation in Poland today, and the U.S. response to it. Ultimately, of course, U.S. policy toward Poland, particularly economic policy, is inseparable from its policy toward the Communist world. For this reason the study focuses in the end on this larger issue.

Indeed, events in Poland have had still wider ramifications. For the Soviet Union, the Polish experience has brought home the lesson that a planned system cannot avoid the laws of supply and demand, and it has sharpened awareness of the need for economic and price reform at home—and of the political difficulties inherent in such reform. It has emphasized to Soviet leaders that, despite their ideological perceptions, economic difficulties in the West are harmful to them rather than beneficial.

⌈ The West, too, has seen once again that planned economies are not immune from balance-of-payment difficulties. More worrisome is the fact that Poland is not the only country that borrowed heavily and then was caught by the doubling of interest rates and the fall in commodity prices.⌉ Consequently, unless economic conditions change, the United States may find its policy toward Poland increasingly caught up in the issues of foreign policy toward the third world. ⌉

The author has benefited from comments on the manuscript by Christopher Bobinski, Daniel L. Bond, Adam Bromke, Alexander Czepurko, Richard T. Davies, Sheila Fitzpatrick, Raymond L. Garthoff, Werner Hahn, John Hardt, Dale Herspring, Edward A. Hewett, William F. Kolarik, Jr., Tadeusz Kowalik, Herbert S. Levine, John D. Steinbruner, Thomas W. Symonds, Jr., Wladyslaw Welfe, and Jerzy Wiatr. It should be emphasized that none are responsible for the analysis in this study—and, least of all, for the policy recommendations, which most of them never saw.

The author is also grateful to Susan E. Nichols, who typed the manuscript; to Caroline Lalire, who edited it; and to Clifford A. Wright, who verified its factual content. The study was supported by a grant from the Ford Foundation.

The views expressed herein are those of the author and should not be ascribed to the Ford Foundation or to the trustees, officers, or other staff members of the Brookings Institution.

BRUCE K. MACLAURY
President

July 1981
Washington, D.C.

The Polish Crisis: American Policy Options

THE POLISH crisis of the last two years has been an intensely emotional experience for the United States. Solidarity's heroic struggle for freedom against great odds captured our imagination, and the imposition of martial law—especially on the eve of Christmas—was a heavy blow. Yet the Polish crisis was a difficult experience for the United States for another reason. American policy toward the Soviet Union and especially toward Eastern Europe has been marked by contradictions and ambiguities, which Poland brought into sharp focus. Since no administration could conceivably satisfy all the conflicting policy goals, every action or inaction has been subject to severe criticism. For this reason, Poland is a perfect case study for an examination of the contradictions in U.S. thinking and policy, the perfect starting point for a clarification of our thoughts about what we can and should do in our foreign policy.

First, of course, Poland provides the severest test of the costs the United States is prepared to incur itself or see inflicted on others in its ideological and economic struggle against the Soviet Union. A Soviet invasion of Poland would have tied down Soviet forces and increased the burden on the troubled Soviet economy—but at a terrible cost to the freedom and economic well-being of the Polish population. Was it an outcome that we would have preferred? In more general terms, to what extent should our policy toward Eastern Europe be an instrument of our policy toward the Soviet Union and to what extent should Eastern Europe be treated as an important region in its own right?

Second, the Polish crisis forces us to think through our assumptions

1

about the long-term stability of the Soviet system and our policy with respect to it. In a rather vague and generalized way, the United States has tried over the years to encourage the Soviet Union and Eastern Europe to become less repressive. But it has also retained a hope—weak among many people, but stronger among others—that the Soviet system might actually collapse. Poland demonstrated that workers can revolt in a Communist country and that the Communist policy of the 1970s of large-scale importation of Western technology on the basis of Western credits is not a solution to the system's economic problems.

Few doubt that in an ultimate crisis the Soviet Union could and would intervene militarily to prevent the collapse of the Polish system. If, however, a similar crisis occurred in the Soviet Union and if the Soviet soldiers refused to fire on demonstrating workers, there are no outside troops that would intervene to save the system. It would fold as completely as the tsarist system did in March 1917, when the Russian troops sided with the bread rioters and could not be used against them.

At a time when a crucial succession is imminent in the Soviet Union that will be fought in large part over how much economic reform to introduce, the West faces crucial choices. Should it adopt the more open, relaxed type of policy that economic reform and gradual liberalization in the Soviet Union is likely to require, or should it try to launch a policy of economic warfare that might scuttle reform but perhaps thereby facilitate the collapse of the Soviet system?

And, finally, the Polish crisis has forced the United States—or, perhaps, it is more accurate to say, should force the United States—to rethink some of its broader assumptions about foreign policy. Whatever the theoretical effect of concerted Western policy on Soviet evolution, the NATO countries and Japan, which have a combined GNP (and a combined number of troops) 1.5 times that of the United States,[1] show little inclination to defer to the United States on critical foreign policy decisions, including economic relations with the Soviet Union and Eastern Europe. The time must come when the United States accepts Europe and Japan as sovereign nations rather than as appendages and designs its response—whatever its nature—in full recognition of that fact. The costs and benefits of an economic policy toward the Soviet

---

1. *The World Almanac and Book of Facts, 1981*, pp. 522–91 passim; and *The World Almanac and Book of Facts, 1982*, pp. 519–91 passim.

Union that is undercut by allied action are very different from those of a policy that is supported by it.

Indeed, the Polish events also raise questions about the general characteristics of American foreign economic policy. The foreign exchange problem was a critical part of the Polish crisis, and the importance of the political criterion in Western economic decisions was a critical part of the exchange problem. Détente provided a political framework conducive to the expansion of loans to Poland. When economic and political difficulties emerged, the most frequent political response was to provide or advocate more credits, even though that exacerbated the foreign exchange deficit. When martial law was declared, the instinctive response was once again economic—only this time it was to impose sanctions as punishment. The impulse to punish was so strong that many Americans were oblivious to the possible consequences of their proposals for the Western financial system or for other underdeveloped countries that are approaching similar financial straits.

An examination of the Polish crisis provides, therefore, a rare opportunity. It permits us to understand the factors that brought a Communist system to the point of collapse and to assess the likelihood of an analogous development in the Soviet Union. It allows us to judge the effectiveness or ineffectiveness of the policy of politicizing economic relations with the Communist world. It clarifies the nature of the dilemmas we face in our policy vis-à-vis the Soviet Union and Eastern Europe and helps us to recognize the hard choices that need to be made. And finally, of course, an understanding of the roots of the Polish crisis may shed some light on the likelihood of Polish recovery in the future and the concrete steps that have the best chance of success in America's policy with respect to Poland specifically.

American Dilemmas

The list of the U.S. goals and interests behind its policy toward Poland has always been a long one. It has included the promotion of greater independence for Poland, the limitation of Soviet power, the preservation of peace in Europe, the promotion of greater freedom inside Poland, the maintenance of contact between members of the Polish community in the United States and their relatives in Poland, grain sales to a potentially important customer, and, increasingly, the protection of the Western financial community from the consequences of financial collapse in Poland.

Since a democratic government in Poland would tend to be anti-Russian and pro-American, the promotion of full democratization would obviously serve many of these goals—if only the policy had a serious chance of success. Indeed, if the Soviet system itself is sufficiently fragile, a revolt in Poland or the strain created by suppressing it could lead to a disintegration of the Soviet Union itself. In the most extreme scenario, some people could argue that democratization would lead not only to a disappearance of the Communist system but also to a decline in Russian power. Many of the non-Russian republics of the Soviet Union might well break away from it. Eastern European countries, it is hoped, would become democratic, and most, if not all, would surely cease to be Soviet military allies. (There are territorial conflicts among Eastern European countries that might lead one or the other side to ally itself with the Soviet Union for expansionist or defensive purposes.)

In the real world, however, such a maximalist scenario has a quality about it of wishful thinking. In practice, the United States has encountered many dilemmas in pursuing the various goals behind its Polish and Eastern European policy. First, of course, it has not been clear whether a maximalist strategy would work in Eastern Europe and, if not, whether its failure would interfere with the achievement of less sweeping goals. In recent years most of the Eastern European countries—including, of course, Poland—have been deviating increasingly from the Soviet model, and the Soviet Union might well permit even greater autonomy in these countries if it came slowly. On the other hand, as the case of Czechoslovakia demonstrated, change that is too radical may produce a Soviet intervention and may result in years of greater repression or conformity.

In these circumstances, should the United States try to encourage unrest in Eastern Europe in the hope that it will increase the pressure for reform, or should the United States fear that any unrest will go so far as to provoke repression? If the United States provides aid to those countries that are changing, where is the dividing line on meaningful reform? After all, even Bulgaria, the most conformist of the Eastern European countries, has made some interesting changes in the relationship between industry and agriculture. A loose definition of change could lead to aid for all of Eastern Europe.

A second and related dilemma involves the American desire for internal evolution in Eastern Europe and the desire for those countries to have a foreign policy independent of the Soviet Union. In practice, the countries that have changed the most rapidly internally—Hungary and Poland—are quite loyal to the Soviet Union in foreign policy. The country with the most independent foreign policy—Romania—has had one of the most repressive regimes. If the United States provides aid on the basis of either domestic conditions or foreign policy, does it not reinforce the status quo in the other area? For example, does not economic reward for Romanian foreign policy independence strengthen Romania's ability to maintain internal suppression?

A third dilemma involves a possible conflict between the break-up of the Soviet bloc and the maintenance of peace in Europe. Europe has been peaceful for thirty-five years. Whenever any change is considered—transformation of NATO, renunciation of the first use of nuclear weapons, withdrawal of American troops from Europe, independence for Eastern Europe—the thought always has to arise: can one be certain that the change will not somehow lead to an unraveling of peace in Europe? Obviously, such an argument could paralyze any policy that would change anything, but a thorough disintegration of the Eastern European system would challenge Soviet interests in the most direct way. For understandable reasons, the idea that the West has an interest in stability in Eastern Europe only surfaces occasionally in public. But no one has ever witnessed a case in which a nuclear power begins to disintegrate, and there is always a natural human tendency not to want to tamper with success. The generation that remembers the havoc wreaked in Europe from 1914 to 1945 may make peace a high priority.

A fourth dilemma—or, rather, set of dilemmas—concerns U.S. economic interests. The United States is a major exporter of grain and coal, and its banks are deeply involved in the extension of international credit. Poland is a major exporter of coal and in recent years has been a major importer of grain and credits. The quantities involved are not huge from the American perspective, so that their importance does not loom as large as American grain sales to the Soviet Union or European credits to Poland. Nevertheless, there are certain to be some people in the United States who have considered that a disruption of Polish industry and trade might increase American coal sales to Europe. There are certain to be others who have favored American credits to Poland to buy grain, even if this might deepen the Polish financial crisis. There are still others whose only priority is to have their loans repaid. In broader perspective, these economic interests tend to cancel each other out, for in the long run the Poles will not be able to buy grain or pay back the loans if they do not export coal, but in the short run the individual economic pressures may have an impact.

The fifth and most important dilemma facing U.S. policymakers is the conflict between greater independence for Eastern Europe as a national interest or human rights goal in itself and Eastern European policy as an instrument of policy toward the Soviet Union. Here too, as has been seen, the conflict is far from complete. In general, the Eastern European evolution is going to parallel the Soviet evolution. If the Soviet Communist system collapses, so will the Eastern European; if the Soviet system becomes more liberal, so on the average will the Eastern European systems; and if the Soviet system becomes more Stalinist, the Soviet leaders will surely crack down on Eastern European deviation as well as on that at home.

Nevertheless, circumstances exist in which this conflict of goals can become severe. To make matters worse, one can make opposing arguments about the nature of the conflict, depending on one's assumptions about the Soviet Union and the priority of American goals with regard to it.

One possible argument is that change in the Soviet Union is possible and that change in Eastern Europe will promote it. In the words of Zbigniew Brzezinski in 1965:

> Détente inevitably challenges Soviet control over East Europe. . . . Only in a relaxed international atmosphere could the hidden tensions and contradictions that plague the East surface and become politically important. . . . Individual defections [of the East European states to the West] would reduce the moderating influence of East Europe on Russia, and thus decelerate the ultimately crucial process of Russian evolution.
>
> The more desirable sequence of change would begin with the internal liberalization of the East European societies and lead toward their gradual evolution into a Greater Europe jointly with the Soviet Union. . . . Thus, East Europe, while not breaking away from the Soviet Union, may pull the Soviet Union forward by moving ahead of it, thereby cumulatively preparing the ground for a better East-West relationship.[2]

It could well be argued that this prediction was essentially accurate, if perhaps more long term than anticipated. During most of the Brezhnev

---

2. Zbigniew Brzezinski, *Alternative to Partition* (McGraw-Hill, 1965), pp. 121, 136–37. The order of the first two sentences has been reversed.

period, a number of events reduced the need for the Soviet leaders to consider serious reform,[3] but now the problems that Brezhnev has been sidestepping have piled up. In 1981 Leonid Brezhnev for the first time told a party congress that many valuable experiments were taking place in Eastern Europe and that the Soviet Union should learn from them and adopt some of them.[4] Especially after the Polish revolt, the pressure on the Soviet leaders to adopt Hungarian-like reform has increased strongly, and at least partial movement in this direction seems probable during the succession. (The selection of Yuri Andropov as Mikhail Suslov's successor as Central Committee secretary may be a favorable sign in this respect.) Since economic reform in the Soviet Union would require the same type of price rises needed in Poland and might well lower the priority for military spending as the leadership searches for money for compensatory wage increases, it might, indeed, prepare the ground for better East-West relations.

A contrasting argument is that the same factors which are pushing the Soviet Union toward reform and which might produce a significant evolution of the country in the 1980s make the Soviet system fragile and that added pressure could now shatter it. From this perspective, a Soviet invasion of an Eastern European country—especially one as populous as Poland—might increase the financial strain on the Soviet economy and increase the possibility of Soviet collapse. In addition, one might suggest that a Soviet invasion of Poland—especially a bloody invasion— would tie down Soviet troops and strengthen anti-Soviet feelings in Western Europe (including Western Communist parties). This argument could have been particularly strong in 1980 and 1981 because of the crises in Afghanistan and Iran. If it was feared that the Soviet Union was seriously considering an attack on the Persian Gulf, then involvement in Poland would surely end that threat. If one was determined to punish the Soviet Union economically for Afghanistan, then the shipment of grain to Poland might directly or indirectly relieve the Soviet burden. This latter consideration remains relevant in 1982 as well. If one is pursuing a policy of economic warfare against the Soviet Union for

3. These included a sharp rise in the price of gold and petroleum (two major Soviet export items), the availability of Western credits, and the coming of age of the members of the postwar baby boom (which meant a massive influx of well-educated youth into the labor force).

4. *Pravda*, February 24, 1981.

whatever reason, then the worse the economic conditions in Eastern Europe, the better from this perspective.

These differing arguments can lead to different dilemmas. If the central concern is internal change in Eastern Europe, then one faces the question, already discussed, about the desirability of aid to Romania and of a policy of stimulating maximum unrest. If one is interested in putting pressure on the Soviet Union, then the question centers on the human rights and independence of Eastern Europe. Whatever foreign policy goals a Soviet invasion of Poland might promote, it would not be pleasant for the Poles.

The Historical Response to Dilemmas

Faced with many pressures in its policy toward Eastern Europe, the United States has historically responded to each of them in a half-hearted way. It did not recognize the major border changes resulting from World War II until it supported the Bonn-Warsaw Treaty of 1970, and even then the support was muted. It continually gave verbal support to Eastern European independence, even sponsoring such events as "Captive Nations Week." Besides its regular Voice of America broadcasts, the United States established a Radio Free Europe to report more directly on events in Eastern Europe itself. Since Radio Free Europe was concentrating on materials and conclusions not found in the official press, its main result—if it was successful—was to make the local citizens more dissatisfied with their regimes than they otherwise would be. It was described by the director of Voice of America as "the voice of free East Europeans speaking to their captive homeland,"[5] and as dissident movements became more open, Radio Free Europe became an important channel of communication between the dissidents and the local population.

Yet despite these gestures toward a maximalist position, no U.S. administration has indicated that it was willing to use military force to support an uprising in Eastern Europe. Indeed, after Radio Free Europe made some broadcasts in 1956 that could be interpreted as encouraging the Hungarians to revolt, every U.S. administration has made certain that the Eastern Europeans were under no illusions about the possibility

5. Quoted in Bennett Kovrig, *The Myth of Liberation* (Johns Hopkins University Press, 1973), p. 261.

of concrete U.S. aid in the case of a future uprising. Even if the suppression of a revolt would be damaging to broader Soviet foreign policy interests, the United States did not want to assume the responsibility of provoking it directly.

Similarly, no U.S. administration has ever been seriously willing to consider the kind of diplomatic move that might transform Soviet control of Eastern Europe. A reunited, neutral Germany is the key to any basic transformation in Eastern Europe, especially a country in Poland's position. Yet every administration has consistently promoted the rearmament of West Germany, a program that, however commendable on other grounds, has made German reunification even less likely than it would otherwise have been.

In general terms, all administrations have tried to follow a differentiated policy that encourages Eastern European countries to become more independent of the Soviet Union either in their internal or foreign policy. When the Polish Communist leadership successfully resisted Soviet pressure in October 1956 and introduced important domestic changes, Secretary of State John Foster Dulles immediately spoke of possible economic aid, and, in practice, the United States provided Poland with credits and low-interest loans worth $588 million over the next seven years.[6] In 1960 the Kennedy administration granted Poland most-favored-nation status, and a number of goods were gradually removed from the export control list insofar as Poland specifically was concerned.[7] All subsequent American presidents until Ronald Reagan enunciated a similar policy. In 1964 the Johnson administration moved to decontrol the same items for Romania when it became more independent of the Soviet Union in its foreign policy (while remaining orthodox and repressive in its internal policy.)[8]

Nevertheless, the United States has not followed a consistent policy toward Eastern Europe in practice. Congress, which was dubious about trade with Communist countries, passed a series of restrictive laws in 1962–63 that prevented the extension of most-favored-nation status to other Communist countries, including Romania. Moreover, although

6. See Stephen S. Kaplan, "United States Aid to Poland 1957–1964: Concerns, Objectives, and Obstacles," *Western Political Quarterly*, vol. 28 (March 1975), pp. 147–66. The figure is from p. 147.

7. Thomas A. Wolf, *U.S. East-West Trade Policy* (Lexington Books, 1973), pp. 72–73.

8. Ibid., p. 94.

Hungary was beginning to become more liberal, the measures taken and the demands made in the aftermath of the 1956 revolution (notably that all political prisoners be released) prevented even the exchange of ambassadors until 1967. The Vietnam War strengthened the congressional reluctance to deal with allies of the enemy, and the credits to Poland were ended. In 1966, a year in which Western European exports to Eastern Europe had risen to the $3 billion level, the total of American exports was only $153 million.[9]

Basically, the United States had concluded that it could do relatively little to affect Eastern European political development in the short run and that its economic interests in that region were not crucial. Yet at the same time Eastern Europe had a considerable ideological and emotional importance. The result, as Andrzej Korbonski expressed it, was a recognition that "East Europe spelled trouble" and that "one tested method of avoiding trouble is to do nothing or, at least, very little."[10]

With the end of the Vietnam War, the West German recognition of East Germany and the Oder-Neisse border between Poland and Germany, and the development of détente with the Soviet Union, American policy toward Eastern Europe loosened up somewhat. President Nixon was able to give Poland and Romania access to Commodity Credit Corporation and Export-Import Bank credits. And in 1975 a summit meeting of the Conference on Security and Cooperation in Europe in Helsinki recognized—to be sure, not in a treaty, but in a nonbinding agreement—the inviolability of the borders established by World War II. The Helsinki Accords did not, as is frequently alleged, say anything about the legitimacy of the regimes in power in Eastern Europe, but they did imply an acceptance of the incorporation of the Baltic States into the Soviet Union, the Soviet seizure of territory from Poland, Hungary, and Romania in 1939–40, and the compensation of Poland with territory taken from Germany. (Nearly a third of Poland's present territory was part of Germany before 1945.)

The center of the new relationship with Eastern Europe was a rapid movement from economic warfare to "an explosion of East-West trade and Western lending to Eastern Europe."[11] Banks became almost

9. Kovrig, *Myth of Liberation*, pp. 244–45, 265.

10. Andrzej Korbonski, "The United States and East Europe," *Current History*, vol. 64 (May 1973), p. 194.

11. Richard Portes, "East Europe's Debt to the West: Interdependence is a Two-Way Street," *Foreign Affairs*, vol. 55 (July 1977), pp. 751, 771–72.

euphoric about their ability to find a profitable and apparently safe place to invest some of their new petrodollars, but the Western governments were also supportive, either indirectly or with loan guarantees and credits. Reliable figures are difficult to obtain, but the total debt of the Soviet Union and Eastern Europe to the nonsocialist world was approaching $70 billion by the end of the 1970s.[12]

Even in the age of détente, however, the United States remained more ambivalent about the relationship with Eastern Europe than did the countries of Western Europe. The commitments of the American banks were smaller than those of the European banks, and the U.S. government concentrated its attention on two countries that were showing independence from the Soviet Union: Romania and Poland. Even here it was only after Poland erupted in 1976 that the American credits really became substantial.

Prelude to Crisis

Poland has long been an uneasy member of the Soviet bloc. Indeed, it had been the most troublesome province of the Russian Empire, with large-scale revolts in 1830 and 1863 and unrest at other times. The legitimacy of the Communist regime was never widely accepted after it was imposed in 1945, and the Catholic Church remained an organized focus of nationalist sentiment. In 1956 strikes and demonstrations led to a showdown with the Soviet Union, resulting in changes inconceivable during the Stalin period (including a substantial decollectivization of agriculture). In 1970 an attempt by the regime to raise food prices led to an outbreak of strikes, in which many workers were killed.[13] In the aftermath, the price increases were rescinded, and the man who had become party leader in 1956, Wladislaw Gomulka, was removed.

As a result of the 1970 strikes, the new leadership, headed by Edward Gierek, decided that the solution to the Polish problems was a massive industrial modernization program. In the period 1971–75, investment increased by 21.9 percent a year,[14] and as in the classic Stalin formula,

12. Data from the Wharton Econometrics Forecasting Associates.
13. See George Blazynski, *Flashpoint Poland* (Pergamon, 1979), pp. 6–31.
14. Zbigniew M. Fallenbuchl, "The Polish Economy at the Beginning of the 1980's," in *East European Economic Assessment*, pt. 1: *Country Studies, 1980*, Joint Committee Print, a compendium of papers submitted to the U.S. Joint Economic Committee, 97 Cong. 1 sess. (Government Printing Office, 1981), pp. 36–37.

investment was concentrated in heavy industry. Unlike Stalin, however, Gierek strove for a rapid improvement in living standards at the same time that he dramatically raised the level of investment. Moreover, he was even more extravagant in his claims for future rises in the standard of living.

To avoid a choice between investment and consumption, Gierek took advantage of the opportunities presented by détente and heavily used the newly available Western credits—first of all, to finance the importation of Western technology. The annual amount of imports from the nonsocialist countries rose from $1.1 billion in 1970 to $6.8 billion in 1975. While the foreign trade account with nonsocialist countries remained in essential balance in 1971 and 1972, it then fell into severe deficit: $1.3 billion in 1973, $2.1 billion in 1974, $2.7 billion in 1975, and $2.9 billion in 1976. The deficits were covered by loans, and by the end of 1975 the debt to nonsocialist countries had risen to some $7 billion or $8 billion.[15]

Growing Economic Problems

The initial results of Gierek's program were impressive. Not only did the rate of industrial growth accelerate rapidly, but real income rose 40 percent from 1971 to 1976. The most dramatic improvement occurred in meat consumption. The population ate 49.2 kilograms of meat per capita in 1965, 53.0 kilograms in 1970, and 70.3 in 1975. (To understand the significance of these figures, one might note that per capita British meat consumption fell from 50.4 kilograms in 1970 to 46.2 kilograms in 1975.)[16]

Beneath the surface, however, serious problems were building up. One was the growing foreign debt. The figure was not impossibly large in 1975, but the consistent growth in the deficit was alarming—as were many of the reasons for it. To be sure, the Polish difficulties resulted to some extent from unexpected market difficulties. The severe recession of 1974–75 in the West seriously affected demand for Poland's major exports (notably coal and copper), and the 1973 petroleum price rise by

---

15. Ibid., p. 65.

16. P. G. Hare and P. T. Wanless, "Polish and Hungarian Economic Reforms—A Comparison," *Soviet Studies,* vol. 33 (October 1981), p. 492. The authors state that the British and Soviet definitions of meat and meat products are identical. Here, as elsewhere, there are undoubtedly problems in Polish official data, but even if they are exaggerated in detail they point in the correct direction.

the Organization of Petroleum Exporting Countries (OPEC) was partially reflected in a doubling of the price that Poland paid the Soviet Union for its petroleum. At the same time, Great Britain's entry into the European Community in 1974 was accompanied by—one might say, paid for by—increased agricultural tariffs, which hit at another Polish export.[17]

Nevertheless, while the Western recession was temporary, the rise in oil prices and the agricultural tariffs were not. In addition, there were inherent flaws in Gierek's plan. The original program had been naive about the contribution that the new technology could make without the economic reforms that would force the managers to use it. In addition, it had been too optimistic about the speed with which the new capacity would be brought on line and produce export items. (Fearing that the investment bonanza might not last, the ministries had tried to start as many projects as possible. They thought that a half-completed project would have a much stronger claim on resources in a time of retrenchment than a new one.)

Most important, the bulk of the investment had been focused on plants that manufactured finished products; little effort had been made to develop domestic suppliers of intermediate products or raw materials. Thus much of the technology bought from the West was designed to use raw materials obtainable only from the West. For example, a television tube plant used RCA parts, a toothpaste factory needed Western chalk, and much machinery required specialized Western steel. Hence if anything went wrong with exports, these plants would still require hard currency imports to function.

Besides the foreign exchange deficits, a severe inflationary problem was developing inside Poland. Farmers were being given higher prices for their products, and a partial economic reform in 1973 had given enterprise managers the right to award "productivity" bonuses, a system that was apparently functioning with few controls.[18] As a Polish economist was later to explain in private, Poland had given up the strict controls of the old planned system but had not adopted the controls imposed by the market. As a result, nominal money income increased from 473.4

17. For a good summary of the sources of Poland's problems, see Gary R. Teske, "Poland's Trade with the Industrializing West: Performance, Problems, and Prospects," in *East European Economic Assessment*, pt. 1, pp. 84–89.

18. "A Message for the Wogs," *Economist*, August 13, 1977, p. 76. For a good summary of the reform, see P. T. Wanless, "Economic Reform in Poland, 1973–79," *Soviet Studies*, vol. 32 (January 1980), pp. 28–57.

billion zlotys to 883.0 billion zlotys in the 1971–75 plan period—an increase of 410 billion instead of the planned 120 billion.[19] Price rises in some spheres of the economy absorbed some of this increase in purchasing power, but the money supply continued to grow.

The rise in excess purchasing power interacted disastrously with the policy of freezing meat prices. As noted, per capita meat consumption rose from 53 kilograms in 1970 to more than 70 kilograms in 1975, but it was impossible for the regime to keep meat on the store shelves. The population was eating better but becoming increasingly dissatisfied by the shortages. Moreover, the growth in the number of animals required a steady increase in grain imports (the government failed to take the necessary steps to expand feed grain production sufficiently), and the poor Soviet harvests of 1973 and 1974 forced the Poles to turn increasingly to the Western markets for their grain and to use foreign currency to buy it. Those concerned with the growing foreign trade deficits had to be alarmed at the meat problem.

On June 24, 1976, the Polish leaders tried to deal with their problem by raising meat prices by an average of 69 percent and a number of other agricultural prices by varying amounts. Riots broke out in several Polish towns, and a general strike seemed imminent.[20] The price increases were immediately suspended, and now the leaders were in real trouble. They had shown that they were afraid to carry out the needed price reforms, but the basic economic problems remained uncorrected. If agricultural production was to increase, the natural policy was to increase the peasants' incentive by increasing the prices paid to them, but this would only widen the gap between the cost of food and the price charged for it. The heightened expectations of the population meant that the absence of improvement would be felt with special bitterness. It is not surprising that when the *New York Times* correspondent Flora Lewis visited Warsaw in September 1976, she found responsible officials speaking with "an urgency that seemed to verge on desperation."[21]

19. Zbigniew M. Fallenbuchl, "The Polish Economy in the 1970's," *East European Economies Post-Helsinki,* Joint Committee Print, a compendium of papers submitted to the U.S. Joint Economic Committee, 95 Cong. 1 sess. (GPO, 1977), p. 852.

20. For a good short summary of the political events of this period, see Adam Bromke, "The Opposition in Poland," *Problems of Communism,* vol. 27 (September–October 1978), pp. 37–51.

21. *New York Times,* September 19, 1976. During this trip, Flora Lewis published several excellent articles based on her interviews. Ibid., September 20, 1976, and September 22, 1976.

The major solution that the Gierek leadership sought for the problems was to cut back on its industrialization program and the importation of machinery. (The share of gross national product going to investment fell from 32 percent in 1975 to 26 percent in 1978, and was planned to be under 20 percent in the 1981–85 period.)[22] It pledged to eliminate the foreign trade deficit by expanding exports far more rapidly than imports. In 1977 it established special commercial shops that sold better cuts of meat at higher prices (essentially at the price charged in the free peasant markets). In that year these stores handled 0.5 percent of the meat being sold; in 1978 this figure may have risen to 8 percent, and in 1979, 19 percent.[23]

The Carter Response

The Gierek changes in policy coincided with a change of administration in the United States. The Carter administration came into power in 1977 with a strong desire to emphasize human rights in its foreign policy. It signaled its commitment to such a policy in Eastern Europe by announcing a program of doubling the capacity of Radio Free Europe just four days before Secretary of State Cyrus S. Vance flew to Moscow for his first crucial arms-control negotiations in April 1977.[24] Moreover, while the former secretary, Henry A. Kissinger, had concentrated attention on Romania, the country the most independent of the Soviet Union in foreign policy, the Carter administration concentrated on the two countries that were undergoing internal evolution, Hungary and Poland.

In 1977 Hungary was granted most-favored-nation treatment, but it was Poland that received the lion's share of American financial largesse. In June 1977 Poland had $200 million of Commodity Credit Corporation credits outstanding and $143 million from the Export-Import Bank. In 1978 and 1979 Poland was granted an average of over $450 million of CCC credits a year, and the unpaid credits rose to $800 million in

22. Ibid., December 2, 1976; and "Poorer than Last Year," *Economist*, February 16–22, 1980, p. 87.
23. Jan B. de Weydenthal, "Workers and Party in Poland," *Problems of Communism*, vol. 29 (November–December 1980), p. 5.
24. *New York Times*, March 23, 1977. This money went to increase the power of the transmitters. The actual staff of Radio Free Europe, which had been cut from 537 to 403 in the last year and a half of the Ford administration, was not increased in the Carter period. (See the annual reports of the Board for International Broadcasting.)

December 1979. In June 1980, 37 percent of the worldwide total of CCC outstanding credits were held by Poland and another 7 percent by Romania and Hungary combined.[25]

The reason for the emphasis on Poland in U.S. credit policy is not clear, all the more so since it was precisely the agricultural credits and purchases that were one of the final nails hammered into the Polish financial coffin. Cutting back on investment after 1976 meant that export earnings and loans were no longer being used to buy foreign technology (which at least would have given hope of recouping the loans), but were being used for current consumables—raw materials for industry and agricultural products for the consumer—and, increasingly, for debt repayment. In particular, the total agricultural imports from the nonsocialist world rose from $0.5 billion in 1970 to $1.0 billion in 1975 and over $1.5 billion in 1978. By the latter year agricultural imports were about equal to the total trade deficit with the West. Even if agricultural exports are subtracted from imports, the net agricultural deficit constituted 30 percent of the total deficit in the 1976–78 period.[26]

At first the credit policy of the Carter administration was presumably motivated by a desire to help the Polish government reduce popular discontent with the food shortages after the 1976 riots. Then, as it became clear that the credits were of dubious use and might never be repaid (a point that many Treasury Department and Agriculture Department officials began making in opposing them on the scale being suggested),[27] the administration realized that a U.S. refusal of loans would be a signal to the entire Western banking community of the precarious nature of the Polish financial situation and would probably result in other countries reducing their loans. The administration did not want to be the one responsible for bringing down the house of cards.

Economic and Political Deterioration

A house of cards it was. In 1977 a perceptive article in *Foreign Affairs* placed 1980 as the year by which Poland would almost surely have to

25. These figures are drawn from the quarterly reports of the U.S. Department of Treasury, Office of the Assistant Secretary for Economic Policy, *Status of Active Foreign Credits of the U.S. Government.*
26. William J. Newcomb, "Polish Agriculture: Policy and Performance," in *East European Economic Assessment,* pt. 1, pp. 100–01.
27. Some Agriculture Department officials also preferred loans to non-Communist countries, because, unlike Poland, such countries would often make a purchase larger

reschedule its debt, stating that only "a very large increase in the price of copper would offer any real hope" that the debts could be repaid.[28] Nevertheless, the loans continued to be made. The Polish trade deficit with nonsocialist countries was estimated at $2.9 billion in 1976, $2.2 billion in 1977, $1.8 billion in 1978, and $1.4 billion in 1979. The level of debt to the nonsocialist world rose from $7.4 billion in 1975 to $19.6 billion in 1978.[29] As Western interest rates began to increase, the difficulty in servicing the debt increased even more rapidly.

The official statistics that the Polish regime furnished Western bankers in 1980 were very disturbing. Hard currency exports in 1979 were put at $6.7 billion and imports at $8.4 billion. In addition, Poland had a $1.1 billion deficit in its service and remittance account (including interest), leaving a $2.8 billion total deficit in its current account balance. In 1980 it was obligated to repay $5.2 billion in debt principal and $1.9 billion in interest—68 percent of the estimated 1980 exports and service-remittance inflows, but nearly 85 percent of the actual 1979 figures.[30]

The restrictions on investment and the growing foreign exchange problem resulted in a deterioration of the economic situation in Poland during the second half of the 1970s. The rate of growth of socialist industry fell from 10.9 percent in 1975, to 8.6 percent in 1977, to 5.8 percent in 1978, and to 2.8 percent in 1979.[31] With agriculture suffering several bad harvests, meat consumption essentially leveled off; nevertheless, shortages in the stores continued to become more severe. Despite the partial price increases, the subsidy to agriculture continued to rise, reaching $7.6 billion (250.6 billion zlotys) in 1978. By 1980 it came to equal 25 percent of the budget, as opposed to 15 percent in the mid-1970s.[32] The gap between income and expenditures continued to widen, and the amount of excess purchasing power in the hands of the population to swell.

In addition, there were many signs that the population was becoming

than the size of the loan. Certainly the seriousness of the Polish situation was known. See Central Intelligence Agency, National Foreign Assessment Center, *The Scope of Poland's Economic Dilemma: A Research Paper,* ER 78-1034ou (GPO, 1978).

28. Portes, "East Europe's Debt to the West," p. 768.

29. Fallenbuchl, "Polish Economy at the Beginning of the 1980's," p. 65.

30. *Financial Times* (London), August 13, 1980.

31. *New York Times,* December 15, 1981.

32. Allen A. Terhaar and Thomas A. Vankai, "The East European Feed-Livestock Economy, 1966–85: Performance and Prospects," in *East European Economic Assessment,* pt. 2: *Regional Assessments,* p. 573.

more and more discontented. Throughout the 1970s the Catholic Church became more assertive about building churches (the future pope even led the construction of one in Nowa Huta against the wishes of the regime), about teaching the catechism to the young and philosophy to teenagers, and apparently about associating itself with social causes at the parish level, especially among younger priests.[33] The election of a Polish pope in 1978 was not only a testament to the vitality of the Polish church and its support among the population but also a catalyst further strengthening the position of the church as a Polish national symbol.

The sense of social injustice was also rising, with the population focusing less on improvements over the past than on the gap between Gierek's promises and reality.[34] That the strikes and riots of 1976 centered on the meat question, despite the dramatic increase in meat consumption, was symptomatic of the problem. Even though the standard of living had been improving sharply under Gierek (the period 1973–76 alone saw an increase in household expenditures of 17 percent a year for manual workers), 40 percent of the manual workers who were asked in a poll, "Did the living conditions of you and your family generally improve during the years 1970–78?" said there was no change or a deterioration.[35] Similarly, even though the differences between the wages of managerial-technical personnel and those of workers narrowed significantly in this period (the ratio stood at 161:100 in 1965, 138:100 in 1975, and 129:100 in 1979),[36] the regime received little credit. The relative position of unskilled workers and lower-white-collar employees deteriorated, yet

33. Jacques Rupnik, "Dissent in Poland, 1968–78: The End of Revisionism and the Rebirth of the Civil Society," in Rudolf L. Tőkés, ed., *Opposition in Eastern Europe* (Johns Hopkins University Press, 1979), pp. 86–92; and Adam Bromke, "Catholic Social Thought in Communist Poland," *Problems of Communism*, vol. 24 (July–August 1975), pp. 67–72.

34. This point is emphasized by the American ambassador to Poland at the time, Richard T. Davies. Indeed, he suggests that, as a result, "Polish workers believe the socialist state owes them a living." R. T. Davies, "Politico-Economic Dynamics of Eastern Europe: The Polish Case," in *East European Economic Assessment*, pt. 1, p. 16.

35. George Kolankiewicz, "Poland, 1980 under 'Anomic Socialism,'" in Jan F. Triska and Charles Gati, eds., *Blue-Collar Workers in Eastern Europe* (London: Allen and Unwin, 1981), pp. 142–43.

36. Henryk Flakierski, "Economic Reform and Income Distribution in Poland: The Negative Evidence," *Cambridge Journal of Economics*, vol. 5 (June 1981), pp. 142–43. The author concludes that there was some increase in the overall level of inequality from 1972 to 1978 (which brought it back to the 1967 level), but the industrial workers do not seem to have suffered. Ibid., p. 138.

the most explosive strikes were to occur among the skilled workers who were doing well. The population clearly had a basic distrust of the authorities—a general sense of their illegitimacy—that transcended specific grievances.

In this framework, political dissent became more open. Some fifty workers were tried and sentenced for their participation in the 1976 riots, but the Committee to Defend the Workers (KOR) was formed to pressure for their release. Within nine months all but five of the workers were in fact quietly freed. KOR continued to function, however, and other groups arose to join it. In the words of a leading Western observer, the months after June 1976 saw "the emergence of a fundamentally new political situation in the country. Opposition, which in the past had been largely passive and scattered, has now become active—it has taken an organized, vocal, and increasingly political form."[37]

The regime frequently harassed the dissidents with temporary arrests, house searches, and so forth, but dissident activity continued to flourish. When a new group was formed in September 1979 with an explicit program for ending Soviet domination, the police simply watched while speakers denounced Moscow before a crowd of 3,000.[38] A "flying university" continued to function, and a man who had been fired after the 1970 strikes, Lech Walesa, was only one of those who were able to function as an organizer in the Free Baltic Trade Union Movement.

No doubt in part because the regime was generating increasing contempt by its unwillingness or inability to take meaningful action, many Poles were developing the feeling that anything was possible. The number for whom the Soviet actions of 1945 were a dominant memory was gradually declining, while the number whose main political memory was the Soviet retreat in 1956 and the retreat of the Polish leadership in 1970 and 1976 was increasing. This mood was no doubt also intensified by President Carter's human rights program, the election of a Polish pope, the rise to power in Washington of a national security adviser of Polish extraction, Zbigniew Brzezinski, who was challenging the Russians, and the selection of another Polish-American, Edmund S. Muskie, as secretary of state. Many young people, Polish public opinion polls were reportedly revealing, were becoming increasingly aware that Poland would be a battleground in any nuclear war, and some were expressing their anxiety in such terms as "We soon will all be dead.

37. Bromke, "Opposition in Poland," p. 37.
38. "Invisible Limits of Tolerance," *Economist*, September 8, 1979, p. 53.

What does it matter?'' The visit of the pope to Poland in the summer of 1979 produced an outpouring of emotion that was a forerunner of the future.

The Creation of Solidarity

Things came to a head in the spring of 1980. The combination of a weak economy in 1979 and a soaring debt service was finally producing real alarm, especially in the Western financial community. If there had been any hope of postponing the day of reckoning, the Soviet invasion of Afghanistan and the American grain embargo on the Soviet Union ended it. The former raised the sensitivity of the Western bankers to the political risks in Eastern Europe; the latter removed any lingering inclination of the Soviet Union to help Poland with grain sales. In their visits with Polish officials in the spring, the bankers told the Poles that the days of easy credit were over and that something had to be done, specifically including a rise in prices.[39]

The actual outbreak of trouble was touched off by a seemingly insignificant action. As mentioned, since 1977 the leadership had been moving more and more meat from the regular state stores to commercial stores, thereby raising the price of that proportion of the meat supply. On July 1, 1980, the regime shifted pig knuckles, boneless beef, and a few other cuts of meat—a total of 2 percent of the meat on the market.[40] The authorities showed no recognition that political difficulties might result. If they had thought that a serious reaction was likely, they surely would have consulted with the Soviets, who would certainly have counseled a short delay. The Moscow Olympic Games were only three weeks away.

The population's reaction was quite different from what it had been in 1970 and 1976. Almost no demands were made for a reversal of the price increase; instead strikes broke out in many plants over the issue of a compensatory wage increase. The leadership instructed the managers to be conciliatory in granting increases, and it itself did not punish the strike leaders. Wage increases of some 10 to 15 percent were negotiated with the striking workers, and scarce supplies were brought into towns where there were strikes in order to alleviate the shortages.

By failing to punish the strike leaders and by giving the workers raises

39. Juan Cameron, "What the Bankers Did to Poland," *Fortune,* September 22, 1980, p. 125.

40. de Weydenthal, "Workers and Party in Poland," p. 5. See also *New York Times,* July 4, 1980.

after negotiations, the regime was in effect legalizing strikes. If it had had total control of the flow of information, this tactic might have worked, but Poland is a country with rapid word-of-mouth communication. Moreover, KOR was giving continual information about the strikes and about its own program to Western correspondents, which information Radio Free Europe was immediately broadcasting back to Poland.[41] Nonstriking workers knew that not only were they losing wage increases that they could easily obtain but their stores were receiving fewer supplies than those of their more aggressive brethren. The London *Financial Times* noted editorially in late July, "Logically the strikes can only be expected to finish once all Polish workers have been equally compensated for the higher prices."[42] It was a logic that Gierek did not seem to understand.

Until the second week of August, Poland simply faced the problem of short strikes breaking out in one area after another. Then the situation changed qualitatively. Major transportation strikes in Warsaw brought the difficulties dramatically to the attention of the capital, and on August 14, strikes spread to the northern port areas, most notably the Lenin Shipyard in Gdansk, which had been at the center of the 1970 strikes. Specifically, a sit-down strike occurred at the shipyard. In 1970 the workers had been shot at when they moved from the plant to protest the food-price increases. In 1980 they simply locked the plant gate and essentially dared the authorities to come in and evict them.

The dramatic new feature of the northern strike—although also a repetition of the 1970 pattern—was the formation of an Inter-Factory Strike Committee to coordinate the strikes in a number of plants in the region. "Committee" was really a misleading title for this institution, for it had 600 delegates, and its twice-daily deliberations were broadcast on loudspeakers throughout the area. It even temporarily functioned as a quasi-governmental body in running the city.[43] The twenty-one de-

41. The importance of this factor is emphasized in William E. Griffith, "Is Poland Not Yet Lost? A Self-Limiting Revolution?" *Fletcher Forum,* vol. 6 (Winter 1982), pp. 119–20, 122–23.

42. *Financial Times,* July 25, 1980.

43. According to one of the advisers to the committee, "The presidium [of the Inter-Factory Strike Committee] . . . decided which part of the public transport system would work . . . and its commands directed the supply of provisions not only to the striking workers but also to the whole network of food stores in the Gdańsk and Gydnia area." Jadwiga Staniszkis, "The Evolution of Forms of Working-Class Protest in Poland: Sociological Reflections on the Gdańsk-Szezecin Case, August 1980," *Soviet Studies,* vol. 33 (April 1981), pp. 209–10.

mands it issued went far beyond those made by strikers elsewhere. The demands did, of course, include the familiar call for a wage increase, pay for time on strike, and various improvements in services, but many were much broader: to index wages to inflation in the future, to abolish work on Saturdays, "to accept free unions, independent from the party and from employers," "to guarantee the right to strike and safety for all strikers as well as for persons helping them" (that is, intellectual advisers), "to respect the freedom of speech and publication guaranteed by the Constitution," and "to liberate all political prisoners."[44]

At first, the government refused to bargain with the Inter-Factory Strike Committee on the grounds that it included members of the dissident free trade unions and that it encompassed more than one plant. On August 23, however, the government retreated and began serious negotiations, which were led by a Politburo member. On August 30 the Central Committee authorized the negotiator to agree to a freely elected trade union and the right to strike. Most of the other demands were also accepted, at least in hedged form. The government released a number of dissidents from jail, and pledged to give the new trade union and religious programs access to the media, to establish a five-day week, to permit the trade union access to economic information, and (although vaguely) to introduce legislation to reduce the censorship. The trade union representatives for their part promised to recognize the leading role of the party and to limit themselves to economic questions.[45]

On August 31 the agreement between the government and the Inter-Factory Strike Committee was signed on national television. Wearing a crucifix and using a foot-long pen with the pope's picture on it, the leader of the committee, Lech Walesa, became a national hero. Nevertheless, at the party's insistence, the agreement was a purely local one.[46] Strikes were to break out in other regions as workers strove to ensure that they received the Gdansk concessions as well. The actual creation of a nationwide organization—to be called Solidarity, after the slogan of the Gdansk strikes—did not occur until September 18, and its formal

44. The full list of demands are translated in ibid., pp. 222–23.
45. A full description of the development of the strikes in Gdansk, the creation of the Inter-Factory Strike Committee, and the course of its negotiations with the government is found in Neal Ascherson, *The Polish August: The Self-Limiting Revolution* (Viking Press, 1981), pp. 145–94. The text of the Gdansk agreements is translated on pp. 288–89.
46. Staniszkis, "Evolution of Forms of Working-Class Protest in Poland," p. 213. Apparently the party wanted to be "forced" into retreat from below, so that it could not be accused of Dubček-like liberalism from above by the Soviet Union.

registration (and hence official recognition by the government) took place only in early November.

Soviet Interests and Attitudes

The Soviet attitude toward Poland and Eastern Europe in general has had several components. First, it is an amalgam of old prejudices, stereotypes, and historical memories that affect the Soviet elite to some extent as well as the broader population, but the concern for security lies at its base. A man like Brezhnev, who was born in 1906, remembers two major wars on the western border, and Leo Tolstoy's *War and Peace* keeps the Napoleonic invasion fresh in everyone's mind. Although the existence of nuclear weapons reduces the threat of a small country to a large nuclear one, and long-range rockets reduce the value of buffer states, old habits of thought die slowly.

From the point of view of Soviet security, there are of course important differences from country to country in Eastern Europe. The Soviet Union would undoubtedly be concerned about the stationing of nuclear weapons in any of them, but in a conventional war Albania and Yugoslavia in the mountainous and not-so-soft underbelly of Europe present much less of a problem for the Soviet Union than countries on the plain leading to Western Europe. These variations in security interests correspond with Soviet behavior in many ways. The Soviet Union did not intervene when Yugoslavia and Albania left the Soviet bloc in 1948 and 1961, respectively, and it has even tolerated major foreign policy deviation from the Romanians since the 1960s. By contrast, it sent troops into Hungary when that country threatened to leave the Warsaw Pact in 1956; no other country north of Romania has even raised a foreign policy challenge since that time. Even the Solidarity leaders tried to reassure the Soviet Union on this point. This geographical pattern is no coincidence.

The two countries of primary security concern to the Soviet Union are East Germany and Poland. East Germany is a worry not so much because of itself but because of the potential of its being reunited with West Germany. If the Communist regime collapsed in East Germany, the inhabitants would surely choose to adopt the West German political system and to join together in a single Germany. Furthermore, the desire of the Germans for reunification means that East Germany is the one

Eastern European country that a Western power has a potential interest in invading. A country such as the Soviet Union certainly includes people who can convince themselves that the possibility is real, and it has more who wonder what the West German and even the U.S. response might be to a widespread and continuing uprising in East Germany. The United States should never underestimate the ability of Soviet strategists to take improbable threats seriously. After all, it has taken crucial defense decisions on the basis of a Soviet brigade in Cuba and the unlikely possibility of a Soviet first strike on its Minutemen.

As a country of 36 million people (basically two to three times the size of the population of the other Eastern European countries), Poland is significant in its own right, all the more so because it has a territorial grievance against the Soviet Union. As a result of the Soviet-German nonaggression pact of 1939, the Soviet Union occupied the eastern third of Poland when the Germans invaded and incorporated that territory into the Belorussian and Ukrainian republics. The Polish Communist government, of course, ratified the boundary change after the war, and it was further recognized in the Helsinki Accords in 1975. Nevertheless, there is no guarantee that a non-Communist government would adopt the same attitude or that the West would not repudiate the Helsinki Accords on some grounds (say, the nonobservance of the human rights clauses) and support the claims of a non-Communist Poland.

More important, Poland is the pathway to East Germany. In the territorial changes that resulted from World War II, the Soviet Union was able to assure itself of a direct border with all its satellites except Yugoslavia, Albania, Bulgaria, and East Germany. In the period before the war, the Polish government had refused to enter into any collective security measures against Germany that would include the right of Soviet troops to pass through Poland to fight the Germans, a refusal that remains an intense memory within the Soviet foreign policy establishment. Even those Soviet scholars who privately think that the Soviet Union was partly responsible for the cold war cannot see how Stalin could have tolerated an elected government in Poland that might have cut the lines of supply to East Germany. None of the public and private Soviet discussions of the Polish crisis of 1980–81 gave the slightest indication that the Soviets' concern about this problem had lessened or that their attitude toward it had changed.

The second component of the Soviet attitude toward Eastern European countries is concern about their internal evolution. To some extent this concern has overlapped with the security one. In Stalin's world view, a country's foreign policy depended on the nature of its internal system. A government in a Marxist-Leninist socialist society inevitably would be a Soviet ally; one in a capitalist society would, except perhaps for temporary tactical reasons, be an enemy. This feeling has faded with the experience of Albania, China, and Yugoslavia, but the Soviet leaders still seem to fear that they have generated such hostilities in Eastern Europe since World War II that a democratically elected regime might well be anti-Soviet. They indeed have such a worry in the Polish case.

In addition, however, the Soviet leaders worry about internal developments in Eastern Europe because of their possible effect on the Soviet Union itself. Traditional Marxist ideology insisted that the laws of history are as deterministic as the laws of evolution, and the Communist party rested its claim to legitimacy on the assertion that it understood and represented the forces of history. Communist victories have permitted Soviet spokesmen to state that "the victory of socialist revolutions in a group of countries of Europe, Asia, and Latin America, as well as the selection of the path of socialist orientation by a number of countries, is convincing evidence that world history is developing precisely as the founders of scientific communism foresaw."[47] By contrast, if such systems are overthrown, the possibility suggests itself that history is "reversible" and that the regime's ideological base is faulty.

In more practical terms, developments that are tolerated in Eastern Europe as a legitimate part of socialism encourage people in the Soviet Union to push for them as well. If Alexander Dubček's policies were an acceptable form of socialism for Czechoslovakia, then why could not Soviet intellectuals have claimed that they were acceptable for Soviet socialism too? If Polish workers can form their own independent trade union and can strike, then why cannot Russian workers—and Ukrainian and Uzbek workers—demand the same rights? Some radical innovations (for example, decollectivized agriculture in Poland) have not spread, but that only partially reduces the fears of the conservatives.

Nevertheless, it would be wrong to think that there is a single Soviet attitude toward change in Eastern Europe. Those who want no change in the Soviet Union like to legitimate the status quo by claiming it to be the result of firm laws of historical development. And of course if there are firm laws of historical development, all socialist countries must follow them. In this view, therefore, significant deviation must be a mistake and in a sense counterrevolutionary.

47. V. Korionov, in *Pravda*, June 6, 1981.

On the other hand, those who believe that the Soviet Union needs considerable reform want a broader and more flexible definition of historical laws and of socialism—one that, at a minimum, will permit the reforms that they want. For those who know what they want, the existence of such reforms in Eastern Europe may be vital for purposes of legitimization. For others who think that reform is necessary but who are not certain about its content, Eastern European countries can serve as laboratories where various economic and social experiments can be tried out and their value for the Soviet Union determined. Over the years scholars and journalists have studied Eastern Europe in order to draw conclusions from its experience and have advocated analogous policies for the Soviet Union.[48] At the 26th party congress in 1981, even Brezhnev himself said this was necessary:

> The fraternal countries have accumulated a variety of positive experience of organizing production, of administration, and deciding economic problems. We know, for example, how skillfully the work of agricultural cooperatives and enterprises in Hungary is organized and what valuable experience of rationalizing production and economizing energy and raw materials exists in the GDR. The system of social security in Czechoslovakia has not a little of interest and value. Useful forms of agro-industrial cooperation are found in Bulgaria and a series of other socialist European countries. Comrades, let us study more attentively and use more widely the experience of the fraternal countries.[49]

The delegates to the congress applauded.

The crucial question, of course, is: which type of innovation in Eastern Europe is tolerable and even desirable and which crosses the line into the dangerous and the unacceptable? This is as much a subject of disagreement and debate in the Soviet Union as is the future course of socialism itself in the country. There is no question, however, that the Soviet Union was deeply concerned about the course of events in Poland.

The Soviet Response to Solidarity

During the first weeks of the Polish strikes, the Soviet media made no mention of them but also gave no indication that the situation was

48. For an early set of such articles, see those by F. Burlatsky and V. Gerasimov in *Pravda*, June 20, 1966, and June 27, 1966. For recent examples, see ibid., September 7, 1981, and *Literaturnaia gazeta*, March 17, 1982, p. 13. Typical of books that advocate change in the Soviet Union on the basis of Eastern European experience are many of those of Konstantin I. Mikul'sky.

49. *Pravda*, February 24, 1981.

unacceptable. Tass regularly carries a column on Mondays, Wednesdays, and Fridays that features innocuous stories about "countries of socialism." The number of times a country is featured in this column usually varies with its political standing in the Soviet Union. Thus for the period from January 1 to August 18, 1980, a total of 60 stories were found on Bulgaria in this column, 53 on Czechoslovakia, 50 on Poland, 45 on Hungary, 44 on East Germany, 15 on Yugoslavia, 14 on Romania, and none on Albania. From July 1 to August 18, 1980, Poland received the most stories of all.[50]

The situation changed drastically when the Inter-Factory Strike Committee was formed in Gdansk and especially when the Polish leadership began to negotiate with it. Subsequent reports reaching Moscow indicated that reservists had been mobilized almost in panic in the Carpathian military district in the western Ukraine.[51] Even if these reports are inaccurate, one fact is indisputable. August 18 was the last Tass column on the countries of socialism in which Poland was mentioned until at least May 1982. Poland was no longer in as good standing as Yugoslavia.

The day after the Gdansk agreements, *Pravda* carried a long article about Poland by A. Petrov, a pseudonym used for authoritative expressions of view, and it was very negative.[52] Petrov placed emphasis on the "antisocialist elements" in Poland that were making "political demands that reveal their true interests" and that were heavily supported from the outside. Tass reports echoed the theme, even claiming on September 3 that Radio Free Europe was bragging in its broadcasts about "its own 'huge part' in the Polish events."[53]

On September 7 Stanislaw Kania, a long-time Polish party official who had specialized in party work in agriculture before becoming the

50. The Tass column is almost never used by the editors of national newspapers and only sporadically in the republican newspapers. Even then, the newspapers may carry only two or three of the four or five stories normally included in the column. Nevertheless, enough columns are published to ensure that a virtually complete set of them can be assembled. While the count is somewhat incomplete, and small differences, such as that between Yugoslavia and Romania, may well be inaccurate, the omissions should not be significant. The counts for other socialist countries for this period were: Mongolia: 31, Vietnam: 28, Cuba: 26, North Korea: 20, and China: 0.

51. *Financial Times,* February 13, 1981.

52. *Pravda,* September 1, 1980. The London *Times,* which called the Petrov article "an extremely ominous sign," thought the story so important that it ran the story as its lead, putting the article about the Gdansk agreement itself on an inside page. *Times,* September 1, 1980.

53. *Pravda,* September 4, 1980.

head of the Central Committee department and then the Central Committee secretary supervising the security forces and the military, replaced Gierek as the Central Committee first secretary. The Soviet press welcomed his election. It printed a long excerpt from his acceptance speech, which included the argument that the strikes were not against socialism or the party but were the result of serious mistakes by the old leadership. Implicitly, the Soviet leadership was acknowledging that changes were necessary.

What the Soviet media did not suggest, however, was that a freely elected trade union, independent of the party, might be an acceptable part of the necessary changes. In one context or another, Soviet spokesmen repeatedly said that party leadership of the trade unions was necessary, that there should be a unified Polish trade union movement, organized basically like the old trade unions. A *Pravda* review of Lenin's policy toward trade unions did not mention Poland, but it emphasized his attack on the main opposition of his time—"the Workers' Opposition"—and its "anarchist-syndicalist" conception of trade unions. Lenin was quoted as saying that these ideas were "either a bourgeois provocation of the deepest type or an extremely stupid or slavish repetition of slogans of yesterday."[54] In November Konstantin U. Chernenko, Brezhnev's personal assistant and closest associate, used the identical quotation from Lenin in an article in *Kommunist*.[55]

The existence of Solidarity was never directly reported in the Soviet press until late November, and then it was in the context of a report about a threatened railroad strike that, the article emphasized, would harm the defense capability of Poland and halt shipments (read Soviet military shipments) between the Soviet Union and East Germany.[56] Lech Walesa himself was almost never mentioned, but the two times that his name did appear left a chilling impression. One time he was identified as a man engaged in illegal trade union activities before the outbreak of strikes;[57] the second time was worse. Allegedly quoting *Der Spiegel,* Tass reported that Jacek Kuron, the leader of KOR, "tried to direct the actions of the striking workers in Gdansk in a channel favorable to himself. He placed at the head of the workers' movement, Walesa,

54. Ibid., September 25, 1980.
55. K. Chernenko, "Velikoe edinstvo partii i naroda," *Kommunist,* no. 17 (November 1980), p. 16.
56. *Pravda,* November 25, 1980.
57. Ibid., September 7, 1980.

who, in Kuron's words, was only 'a symbolic figure,' while the actual 'brain center' was [KOR].''[58]

The Soviet Union had several fears. In immediate terms, the Soviet leaders were afraid that the unrest would get out of hand. But their basic, long-range concern was that the leaders of an elected trade union would have a legitimacy not possessed by the party leaders. The latter claimed to be the representatives of the proletariat, but if national and regional trade union leaders were actually elected by the workers, they would have a far better claim to that title. Especially in a society in which prices and wages were out of balance and in which the government had found it impossible to impose price increases, the elected trade union leaders would be in a position to determine economic policy. Indeed, if they were to raise questions about censorship, the role of the police, and the removal of local political officials—and if they could back up their demands on these matters with effective strikes—they would come close to being the government itself or at least the power behind it. In addition, of course, if elected trade unions became accepted in Poland, there would be an excellent chance that the demands for them would spread to the rest of Eastern Europe and to the Soviet Union itself. The Soviet sensitivity on this last point was dramatically shown in the decision to jam the Voice of America and other Western broadcasts to the Soviet Union once the Polish regime began negotiating with the Inter-Factory Strike Committee.

Nevertheless, to state that the Soviet leaders found Solidarity unacceptable is not to say that they were certain what to do about it. Poland has over twice the population of Czechoslovakia and over three times that of Hungary, and there were many indications that a Soviet invasion would meet with resistance. Military intervention would require a large number of troops, and there might be guerrilla action for months or even years. One could imagine hair-raising scenarios in which Soviet ships tried to stop fleeing boat people, in which Western ships tried to help them, and in which navies came into conflict.

Moreover, the Soviet Union had other foreign policy goals that might be affected by a full-scale operation in Poland. Soviet troops were in Afghanistan, American ships were in the Persian Gulf because of the U.S. hostages in Iran, and in September a war erupted between Iran and Iraq. If the Soviet troops were tied down in Poland, Soviet freedom of

58. *Krasnaia zvezda,* September 13, 1980. This item was not printed in *Pravda.*

action might be severely limited in these other areas, especially if the United States decided to intervene in Iran or to react to Poland by increasing supplies to the Afghan rebels, or if Israel decided to invade the Soviet ally Syria.

And, far from least, Western Europe was showing a willingness to be independent of the United States on many key issues. A bloody Soviet intervention in Poland would severely test the European commitment to détente. At a time when Eastern Europe was in heavy debt, further European loans for the building of a natural gas pipeline across Eastern Europe would be doubtful. Even though the Soviet Union was denying responsibility for the Polish debt, the risk of a formal default for Polish nonpayment would be much greater if Soviet troops were directly involved.[59]

In 1956 the Polish party had been able to handle the unrest by making quite radical concessions to the workers and then by repudiating many of them. From the Soviet point of view, this would be the ideal outcome even if it involved some limited changes from the status quo ante. (The Soviet press clearly signaled a willingness to accept a greater role for the trade unions in Poland.)[60] Yet if Solidarity became an institutionalized and accepted part of the Polish scene, if it was skillful in the way that it gradually kept expanding its demands, the Soviet Union might find it increasingly difficult to invade, even though the situation was becoming increasingly unacceptable.

With these dilemmas, there must have been differences of opinion within the Soviet leadership and foreign policy establishment on what to do, but the outlines of the debate are only dimly visible in the public press.

Essentially the Soviet Union had to face three questions: (1) Just how much deviation in Poland was tolerable or even desirable, either for its own sake or as a way to solve the Polish economic problems? (2) What would be the effect of time on the Polish political scene? Would unacceptable changes become irreversible or would economic difficul-

59. For a good summary of the potential costs to the Soviet Union in case of intervention, see Seweryn Bialer, "Poland and the Soviet Imperium," *Foreign Affairs,* vol. 59, no. 3 (1981), pp. 534–36.

60. For example, Soviet newspapers carried Kania's claim that "in the fraternal socialist countries, the trade unions occupy a more important position than in Poland and possess wide possibilities"—a statement implying that it was appropriate for the Polish trade unions to be given greater powers than they had had in the past. *Pravda,* October 7, 1980.

Table 1. *Quantity of Coverage of Selected Foreign Stories in the Newspapers of the Soviet Republics, September–December 1980*

Percent of column lines

Republic	Total column lines[a]	Poland	Afghan-istan[b]	Central America	China	Iran[c]	Peace with West[d]
Baltic							
Estonia	23,900	26	5	2	11	22	34
Latvia	31,600	21	7	6	13	22	30
Lithuania	30,500	21	11	7	14	26	21
Western							
Belorussia	20,500	28	10	10	12	17	23
Moldavia	13,600	13	13	7	8	19	40
Ukraine	19,500	29	8	3	9	18	33
Transcaucasian							
Armenia	17,800	22	8	6	13	20	32
Azerbaidzhan	15,200	21	11	3	8	34	23
Georgia	17,500	17	9	3	10	28	34
Central Asian							
Kazakhstan	14,400	20	8	11	10	26	24
Kirgizia	13,300	13	16	7	15	13	36
Tadzhikistan	26,700	17	17	8	18	18	22
Turkmenia	16,100	18	17	5	17	15	27
Uzbekistan	18,200	22	12	4	12	27	23

Sources: The leading Russian-language newspaper in each republic, each of which is the organ of the Republican Party Central Committee: *Sovetskaia Estoniia, Sovetskaia Latviia, Sovetskaia Litva, Sovetskaia Belorussiia, Sovetskaia Moldaviia, Pravda Ukrainy, Kommunist* (Erevan, Armenia), *Bakinskii rabochii* (Azerbaidzhan), *Zaria vostoka* (Georgia), *Kazakhstanskaia pravda, Sovetskaia Kirgiziia, Kommunist Tadzhikistana, Turkmenskaia iskra,* and *Pravda vostoka* (Uzbekistan).

a. The column lines were counted on a story-by-story basis and are subject to some inaccuracy because of counting or classification error. Official communiqués, which are automatically printed in all newspapers (for example, those about Karmal Babrak's visit to Moscow) are excluded, as are a few wholly nonpolitical categories like sports.

b. Includes stories about Chinese involvement in Afghanistan.

c. Includes the Iran-Iraqi war.

d. Includes reports of support for disarmament, of peace negotiations, and of divisions in NATO that imply a lesser threat than would NATO unity. The choice of articles to include here was difficult because many give a picture of the Western threat but add mitigating factors.

ties sap the Polish revolutionary spirit? (3) What priority should be given the Polish crisis relative to other concerns?

The most suggestive evidence of differing opinions about priority is found in the coverage of foreign policy stories in the regional press (see table 1). Most of the stories came from the Tass and, to a lesser degree, the Novosti news agencies. But these agencies carry far more stories than any newspaper can publish. In practice, there are great variations in what the editors select. Although they must sometimes make random decisions, their respective sense of the importance of the stories in terms of the preference of the local party leaders and the concerns of the local population (and the consequent need to influence its thinking) must have an impact. During the fall of 1980 (and afterward) the republican newspapers varied enormously in the attention they gave to the Polish crisis in comparison with other foreign policy problems. (The actual coverage itself ranged from 1,700 column lines in Kirgizia to 7,600 lines in Latvia from September through December 1980.) Since the first secretaries of the Ukraine and Kazakhstan are full members of the Politburo and those of Azerbaidzhan, Belorussia, Georgia, and Uzbekistan are candidate members, it is difficult to believe that these differences were not expressed in that setting as well.

Perhaps most important of all, the army newspaper, *Red Star (Krasnaia zvezda)*, seemed to be strongly indicating in the first months of the Polish crisis that the Middle East was its primary worry and that Poland was a less imminent problem. In the nine weeks before the 1980 U.S. presidential election, *Red Star* gave less coverage to Poland than the newspapers in nine of the fourteen non-Russian republics. By contrast, it gave great emphasis to the Middle East. Perhaps, like the Republicans, it feared that President Carter would have some "October surprise" in the foreign policy realm and that it should not be overcommitted at this time.

Whatever the reason, the Soviet leadership decided to tolerate the situation for the time being. In late October Kania, together with the chairman of the Council of Ministers, visited Moscow for a meeting with Brezhnev that, according to the Soviet report, was marked by "good neighborness" and "comradely solidarity." Brezhnev was explicitly said to have expressed confidence that Poland would be able to solve the problems that faced it.[61] The threat of an invasion temporarily faded into the background.

The Deepening Crisis

If the creation of Solidarity had been followed by a long period of social peace and economic growth, the wait-and-see policy of the Soviet leadership would have left it with few choices. It would have had little reason to complain and over time might well have reconciled itself to a development it originally considered unthinkable. In actual practice the

61. Ibid., October 31, 1980.

Soviet leaders were not to face this problem. The relationship between the Polish authorities and Solidarity was almost continuously strife-ridden, and the economic difficulties that had produced the unrest became progressively greater.

Sources of the Difficulty

One problem was that Solidarity and the authorities were deeply suspicious of each other. The Solidarity leaders, particularly at first, maintained a relationship with KOR that must have greatly disturbed the government, all the more so since KOR was not acting with discretion.[62] When the national Solidarity leaders tried to distance themselves from KOR, many of the editorial personnel of semilegal Solidarity regional publications continued to be political dissidents. Solidarity for its part remembered that many of the concessions granted to workers in 1956 had been severely restricted afterward, and it constantly worried that this pattern would be repeated.

These mutual suspicions were intensified in a bitter conflict that developed in September and October over the Solidarity charter. The Inter-Factory Strike Committee had acknowledged the leading role of the Communist party in the Gdansk agreement, but the Solidarity organizers were loath to include a clause to this effect in their charter. They feared that in the future this clause would be used by the party to institute its control, but the party no doubt thought that Solidarity was retreating from the Gdansk agreements. The eventual compromise—an acknowledgment of the party's leading role in an annex to the charter—satisfied no one, and by early November a newspaperman could report "a sense that events are spinning out of control and heading for disaster."[63]

Another problem was that the leaders and lower officials both in the party and in Solidarity had opposing self-interests. If Solidarity became an institutionalized part of a stable political system, the radicals and

62. Walesa's image in the first weeks was different from that which emerged later. For example, John Darnton, a *New York Times* correspondent in Warsaw, described Walesa in Jekyll-and-Hyde terms. "Walesa's moderate side emerges after he has consulted with church officials, including Stefan Cardinal Wyszynski. . . . The militant Mr. Hyde aspect of his nature becomes dominant after strategy sessions with Jacek Kuron, of KOR, a principal adviser." John Darnton, "60 Days That Shook Poland," *New York Times Magazine*, November 9, 1980, p. 116.

63. Ibid., p. 39.

dissidents in Solidarity and the conservative officials of the old institutions would lose their bases of support. Thus both of these groups had a vested interest in the continuation of turmoil, and both were in a position to create incidents at the local level that stoked the fires which the national party and Solidarity leaders were trying to dampen.

Although most of the workers left the old trade unions to join Solidarity, the former continued to exist. The conflict of interest between their officials and Solidarity was especially intense. Unlike Solidarity, which was organized on a regional basis, the old unions were structured along industry (branch) lines and hence could dominate negotiations with the ministries, but both Solidarity and the old trade unions were able and eager to negotiate with local management. The problem went even further. The old trade unions had had a fairly big role in the administration of social programs, and they disposed of substantial real resources—vacation resorts, passes for them, insurance programs, and the like. The trade union officials naturally had little desire to give up these resources, for they were the major inducement for workers not to relinquish membership. Solidarity for its part, however, had an equally natural belief that the competition for members should be a fair one, and that if it was the major trade union, it should be running these programs.

A third problem was that much of the Polish population remained in a restless, perhaps even semirevolutionary, mood. Such upsurges in feelings tend to have a natural pattern of development, and once established institutions are successfully challenged, emotions seldom subside immediately. In the Polish case, this tendency was intensified by a worsening of the economic problems that had produced the original strikes. Industrial production in 1980 was down 1.3 percent from the 1979 level, but this decline was insignificant in light of the figures that compare 1981 production of socialized industry with that of the corresponding period in 1980: in the first two months of 1981 down 10.0 percent, in the first six months down 12.5 percent, and in the first eleven months down 12.9 percent. The second half of the year was even worse than these figures suggest, for those months were being compared with the troubled months of 1980. In the first six months of 1981, both exports to the West and imports from it were 21.5 percent lower than they had been a year earlier, and this had a progressively strong impact on the import-sensitive industries.[64]

64. *Financial Times*, February 5, 1981, March 30, 1981, and July 29, 1981; and Warsaw Domestic Service, December 14, 1981, in U.S. Foreign Broadcast Information Service,

While industrial production declined, the number of people employed remained virtually unchanged; nominal personal income soared by 18 percent in 1980 and then by an additional 30 percent in 1981. Rising prices absorbed some of this increase, especially in the fall of 1981, but the main increases in prices in the private market only transferred money from city dwellers to farmers. The combination of a large rise in the money supply and a decline in the supply of goods in the stores (11 percent by volume in 1981 alone) led to severe shortages by the summer of 1981.[65]

With so much money available, a hoarding psychology developed, which a marginal increase in supplies could not change. Even the introduction of rationing in April sometimes made the lines longer, for persons who did not use a rationed item (notably cigarettes and alcohol) insisted on their ration so that they could barter it for other goods. In these circumstances, the rural population had no strong incentive to deliver to the market, especially to the state system, which paid lower prices than the private market or the black market.

The reasons for this worsening economic situation were manifold. Of course the strikes and the politicization of the workplace (with the accompanying increase in the number of meetings) had some influence, but probably not as much as appeared on the surface. A more important factor must have been the reduction in the length of the workweek, which occurred in early 1981, because little else explains the minor decline in production in 1980 and the major one that began in 1981 immediately after the five-day week was introduced. The effect of the reduced workweek was not great in most manufacturing industries, for the workers had never averaged a six-day week. (The pattern, as in most Communist countries, was to work little in the first part of the month because of shortages of supplies, but then "storm" in the last days to fulfill the monthly plan.) In the extractive industries the situation was different, particularly in the coal industry.

The coal mines had worked twenty-four hours a day, with each shift having six days on and two off. This system meant that the actual days off for the workers changed from week to week and that they had to

---

Daily Report: Eastern Europe, December 15, 1981, p. G9 (hereafter FBIS, *Eastern Europe*).

65. The statistics in the paragraph are drawn from *Financial Times,* January 21, 1982, and January 30, 1982; and from Warsaw PAP, April 5, 1982, in FBIS, *Eastern Europe,* April 5, 1982, p. G4.

work six Sundays out of eight—a principal source of grievance. The change to a standard five-day week for everyone resulted in the total weekly operation of a mine falling from 168 hours to 120 (29 percent), barring double-time overtime. Coal production fell from 200 million tons in 1979 to 197 million tons in 1980 and to 163 million tons in 1981, which in turn affected not only the performance of other industries but also exports. Total exports of coal dropped from 41 million tons in 1979 to 16 million tons in 1981, those to the West alone from 26 million tons to 8 million tons. This itself caused Poland a loss of over $1 billion in foreign currency.[66]

As 1981 advanced, the factor that loomed largest in the progressive worsening of the economy was the shortage of foreign currency. The new and most productive industrial plants were, as has been noted, built to use Western raw materials, whose purchase had been largely financed by foreign credit. With new credit cut off and export earnings falling, many factories had to curtail production because of the shortages in supplies.

Growing Political Problems

These various elements combined to create a continuous political crisis that worsened even further in the summer of 1981.[67] As one rereads the newspaper reports on the fifteen months between the Gdansk agreements and the imposition of martial law in December 1981, one has the sense of a political order being subjected to Chinese water torture. No sooner was one crisis overcome than another arose on some unrelated question. In September 1980 the problem was the spread of strikes to cities and plants that wanted to ensure that they too received the Gdansk concessions. In October and early November the issue was the registration of Solidarity and the question whether its charter would include a clause about the leading role of the party. A district court arbitrarily included such a clause, and the Supreme Court then permitted it to be placed in the annex. In November the issue was the behavior of the police and the arrest of a printer who leaked a judicial document, with a major Solidarity regional organization calling for a cut in the police

---

66. *Financial Times,* January 7, 1982, and January 26, 1982. The old system of organizing mine work is described in the London *Times,* September 2, 1980, and September 3, 1980.

67. See Ascherson, *Polish August,* pp. 195–277.

budget. In December the focus turned to the struggle for the creation of a rural Solidarity for farmers.

After a brief lull during the Christmas season, January 1981 saw a major crisis about work on Saturday, Solidarity's access to the media, and the rural Solidarity. In February the prime issue was the removal of some provincial political officials, and in March it was the punishment of police who beat up a local Solidarity leader during a sit-in at a provincial government headquarters. In April the long-simmering dispute about the creation of a rural Solidarity was finally settled, but throughout the spring the questions of the police and the trial of right-wing dissidents continually resurfaced.

Basically in the spring, however, the center of attention moved to the Communist party itself. The leadership had decided to hold an extraordinary party congress and to permit a democratic election of delegates to it. Because of the large number of party members enrolling in Solidarity and ferment in other sections of the party, it was possible to imagine that these elections might turn the party into a social-democratic one. Since the Soviet military intervention in Czechoslovakia had been timed to prevent a party congress that would elect a pro-Dubček Central Committee, the possibility of a transformation of the Polish party raised the fears of a Soviet invasion in especially acute form.

In July, as the party congress approached and passed without the feared consequences (this will be discussed later), Solidarity began to prepare for its own first national congress, which was scheduled to open in September. It discussed the contents of its draft program, which included access to the media for Solidarity, controls on the police, and more democratic elections. The main issue, however, was workers' self-management, defined to mean the right of workers to hire and fire the manager. A crisis arose in July over precisely such an action vis-à-vis the head of the LOT national airline. At this time the population was becoming increasingly restive over the growing shortages in the stores and the more severe rationing of meat. August was marked by a wave of wildcat strikes and demonstrations that Solidarity leaders vainly tried to bring under some control, but that also inevitably encouraged the more extreme elements in the union.

Even this list of important issues does not give a proper sense of the turmoil. Various local Solidarity or dissident leaders were continually making statements that were certain to provoke the leadership and the Soviet Union, while the East German, Czech, and Soviet presses issued warning after warning, often expressed in language used before the invasion of Czechoslovakia in 1968. As time passed, Lech Walesa became more and more moderate in his demands, but the fact that his appeals were so seldom heeded—or that they were heeded after his desperate on-the-site intervention or after a crisis punctuated by a Soviet military maneuver—strengthened the impression of chaos.

Almost all the important issues were handled badly by the authorities. The party leaders never seemed to try to meet an issue before it came to a head or to resolve it in a generous and forthcoming manner once it reached a crisis stage. Indeed, they resisted concessions vigorously. But once Solidarity threatened drastic action, they would almost always retreat or at least compromise. This behavior reinforced Solidarity's sense of an adversary that was relentless and ready to counterattack at a propitious moment, while at the same time it gave the extremists the sense that strikes and other radical action could produce results. It must have left the Soviet Union with the feeling that the Polish leadership was hopelessly weak in the face of opposition.[68]

The Party and Solidarity Congresses

Whatever the impetus for change, however, the extraordinary congress of the Polish Communist party in July 1980 marked a turning point in the relationship of the party and Solidarity. The election of delegates to the congress was conducted by new rules that were much more democratic than the old, but the leadership seems to have brought some order into the election process. (An April visit by Mikhail Suslov and a threatening Soviet letter of June 5 played a significant part in this development.)[69] The congress itself passed no radical resolutions.

The surprise of the congress came at the end, in the election of a Central Committee. Central Committees in Communist countries normally contain a high proportion of central and provincial party and government officials, but the Central Committee elected by the 1981

68. As indicated earlier, the provincial Soviet newspapers varied enormously in their decisions on which Tass items on Poland to carry. Only a relatively small number of items were printed in all newspapers. One such, however, was a small story in June that described the postponement of the trial of leading right-wing dissidents. The story was headed "The Regular Retreat," and it must have touched a responsive chord among the editors.

69. *New York Times,* April 24, 1981, June 9, 1981, and June 11, 1981.

Polish congress included only 17 important officials among its 200 full members.[70] There were 279 candidates nominated for the 200 seats on the Central Committee, and prominent officials of both liberal and conservative persuasion went down in defeat. By contrast, all the 80 workers nominated were elected. Apparently the delegates found it easier to choose 79 candidates whom they did not like than 200 whom they did, especially since Kania had not been circulating a slate that he approved.[71] Westerners judged that the newly elected Central Committee members tended to be moderate,[72] but a great many were simply unknowns. Certainly Kania had little reason to rejoice. In the election to the Central Committee, he received only 1,337 votes from the 1,950 delegates, whereas the chairman of the Council of Ministers, General Wojciech Jaruzelski, received 1,615.

The period after the party congress saw some significant developments. First, the regime, while taking no strong action against the various wildcat strikes (except for blocking a protest march on party headquarters in Warsaw), became more resistant to Solidarity demands. As the Solidarity congress approached (it was held in two parts—September 5–10 and September 26–October 8), many of the radical leaders became more extreme in their language, and the Polish press became harsher in its denunciations. Solidarity demanded newspaper space for a reply and backed up its demand with a two-day strike that shut down party newspapers, but the party did not retreat. Solidarity demanded editorial control of the television and radio coverage of its congress and threatened a strike of television workers unless this was done. When the authorities refused, Solidarity backed off from its strike threat. Solidarity did bar television crews from the congress, but this only reduced the coverage. Finally, the authorities refused to permit worker appointment of managers and eventually offered only the right of the workers to veto ministerial nominees for certain unspecified "nonstrategic" plants.

Even more significantly, the authorities became increasingly bellig-

70. The 143 full members of the Central Committee elected in February 1980 included 32 rank-and-file workers and peasants, 84 important officials, and 27 professionals and middle-level managers. The 200 full members elected in July 1981 consisted of 127 rank-and-file personnel, 17 important officials, and 56 professionals and middle-level administrators. (These figures were provided by Werner Hahn.)

71. New York Times, July 21, 1981.

72. Roger Boyes said on the basis of an analysis of its votes that the Central Committee contained 50 to 60 radicals, 30 hard-liners, and 110 moderate centrists. Roger Boyes, "Dogmatic Undertone to Poland's Moderate Politburo," Financial Times, July 21, 1981.

erent and provocative in the way they challenged Solidarity. They announced a tripling of bread, flour, and cereal prices for August 24 and then postponed its implementation for a week—undoubtedly so that it would fall on the anniversary of the Gdansk agreements. Then when the second half of the Solidarity was in session in late September, the authorities announced a doubling of cigarette prices. The timing of these steps was certainly designed to demonstrate to the people the limit of the regime's dependence on Solidarity and the inability of Solidarity to protect them from harsh economic actions.

Second, Solidarity became more radical in its political demands. Although it called for economic moderation—an end to strikes, work on Saturday, and acceptance of the higher bread prices—the Solidarity congress endorsed many proposals that had formerly been associated with the Solidarity radicals: a national referendum on workers' self-management (and a threat to hold one if the government would not); free elections to the national and provincial legislatures, with more than one candidate and with citizen groups free to nominate candidates; public control of the media; revision in the way history was written (that is, honesty in the description of Polish-Russian relations in the past); dismissal of the prosecutor general of the country; and the right to keep foreign passports (that is, free travel abroad). It issued a message to workers in the Soviet Union and other Eastern European countries, pledging support to any who formed their own free trade unions. In the second session of the congress, Solidarity officially called for a reduction in defense expenditures. At the end of the session, Lech Walesa suffered a significant defeat when the delegates elected a 107-man National Commission that was dominated by the radicals. Walesa was able to force through a moderate slate of candidates for the 11-man ruling presidium, but the National Commission remained the final authority.[73]

The reasons for the radical character of the Solidarity congress are not altogether clear. There were many signs that the majority of the Polish people were tiring of radicalism and shortages. As early as April, Walesa had warned in the Solidarity newspaper that "people are tired and do not want more confrontation" and had stated that a turnover of middle-level Solidarity leaders was needed—a replacement of leaders who had come to the fore in the previous summer and who always wanted to fight.[74] Polls showed a steady decline in support for the right

73. *Financial Times,* October 7, 1981, and October 9, 1981.
74. Ibid., April 9, 1981.

to strike and especially for the exercise of this right.[75] Most ominous of all, the celebration of the anniversary of the Gdansk agreements had had to be canceled for lack of popular interest. The authorities' determination to humiliate Solidarity must have rested on a growing confidence that they could get away with it.

Perhaps the explanation for the radical outcome of the Solidarity congress is that the turnover of middle levels of leaders had not occurred and the delegates represented the mood of the previous summer. Very little information is available on the election of delegates to the congress, and none of it suggests that Walesa was conducting organizational work on the lower levels to ensure the election of men who would support him.

It is also possible that many members of Solidarity were becoming enormously frustrated and even desperate. Essentially the only reasonable deal that they could offer the regime—and the Solidarity leadership at least often offered it—was popular acceptance of necessary price increases in exchange for an institutionalization of participation. If the regime was going to be able to make price increases on its own, Solidarity would lose much of its bargaining power. An American analyst sympathetic to the radicals in Solidarity wrote that after the party congress in July the leaders were simply playing a cat-and-mouse game with Solidarity,[76] and perhaps many of the Solidarity activists had the same feeling—that it was now or never, radical political change or none.

Changes in the Soviet Press

Immediately after the Solidarity congress a qualitative change occurred in the Soviet press coverage of Poland. The change in the Soviet army newspaper *Red Star* is particularly interesting in this respect. *Red Star* tends to express military attitudes and frequently can be looked upon as an advocate of the military rather than the official party position, but in times of crisis its editors must take another factor into account. If the Politburo is seriously thinking of using Soviet troops, then the newspaper must prepare the soldiers for action, at least to the extent of making sure that they fully appreciate the severity of the "threat."

75. Ibid., November 27, 1981. In a private meeting in December (the tape of which the government obtained and played), a Solidarity leader stated, "The union is not stronger than it was; it is weaker and every activist realizes it." Some leaders put the number of wavering Solidarity members at 30 percent. *New York Times*, December 13, 1981, sec. 4.

76. Martin Malia, "Poland: The Winter War," *New York Review of Books*, March 18, 1982, pp. 21–25.

Figure 1. *Number of Column Lines of Critical Articles on Poland in* Krasnaia zvezda (*Red Star*), *September 1, 1980, to December 12, 1981*[a]

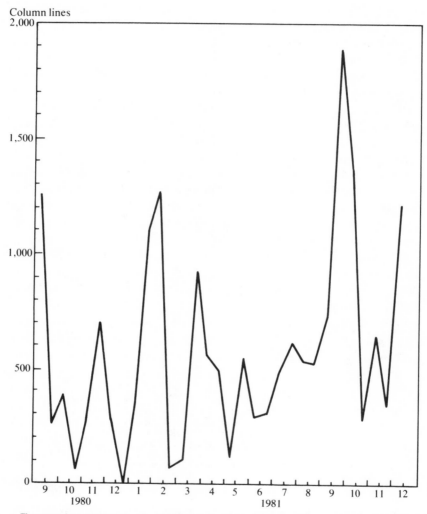

Column lines

a. Three very long speeches given by Stanislaw Kania, Wojciech Jaruzelski, and Victor Grishin (the Soviet representative) at the Polish party congress in July 1981 are excluded.

As indicated earlier, *Red Star* was cautious in its coverage of Poland while the American presidential election was in progress and the Middle East crisis appeared particularly dangerous. Afterward the newspaper shifted to a hard line on Poland, frequently printing the Tass stories that emphasized foreign and KOR involvement in the Polish difficulties. In November and December 1980 several articles seemed to imply that diplomatic concerns should not prevent Soviet intervention.[77] Nevertheless, as figure 1 demonstrates, there were long periods when *Red Star* published only intermittent articles on Poland and when the Soviet leadership cannot have been thinking of imminent intervention. Contrary to the expectations of many Western observers—including me—the longest such period was the three months preceding the party congress.

Even during August 1981, when wildcat strikes were occurring and Solidarity rhetoric was increasingly radical, *Red Star* printed Tass reports about the "intensifying crisis" in Poland but did not give an extraordinary amount of attention to Poland. All this changed after September 9, when the Solidarity congress passed many of its resolutions, including the demand for free elections, and the message to workers in the Soviet Union and Eastern Europe. In the four weeks before September 10, *Red Star* had carried some 795 column lines of negative coverage of Poland; in the four weeks beginning September 10, it carried 3,330 such column lines, a long story every day.

The content of the stories that *Red Star* and other Soviet newspapers were carrying also became more alarming. At the conclusion of the first half of the Solidarity congress, Tass described the session as an "anti-socialist and anti-Soviet orgy" and charged the union with preparing "a seizure of power."[78] Over the next two weeks, the Soviet press published "letters" from workers' meetings at major plants in the Soviet Union rejecting the Solidarity message to Soviet workers and demanding an end to anti-Sovietism. Soviet television presented some coverage of the last such meeting, and the Soviet audience could see the workers holding banners that said, "We will defend socialism in Poland."[79]

The Soviet Party Central Committee itself issued a statement to the

77. See Richard D. Anderson, Jr., "Soviet Decision-Making and Poland," *Problems of Communism*, vol. 31 (March–April 1982), p. 29. The author's suggestion that the generals were in a position to compel Brezhnev to take action on this issue is much less convincing than his suggestion of differences of opinion.

78. *New York Times*, September 11, 1981.

79. Ibid., September 22, 1981.

Poles that was not printed in the Soviet press but was published in Poland. It complained that no one in Poland had been punished for anti-Soviet statements and warned that "further leniency shown to any manifestation of anti-Sovietism does immense harm to Polish-Soviet relations and is in direct contradiction to Poland's obligation to its alliances." It concluded categorically: "We expect that the party leadership and the Government immediately take determined and radical steps to cut short the malicious anti-Soviet propaganda and action hostile to the Soviet Union."[80]

The Imposition of Martial Law

The ultimate outcome of this turmoil was, of course, the imposition of martial law on December 13, 1981. Many Westerners have since debated whether the decision was made by the Polish leaders or was the result of a Soviet ultimatum. To a large extent the argument is artificial. There may well have been differences between the Soviet Politburo and the Polish leaders on what to do at any particular time, as there were within the Polish leadership itself. Nevertheless, the basic interests of the top Polish party elite and of the Soviet Union were similar insofar as Solidarity was concerned. A Solidarity that assumed any dominant political or economic policymaking role was as much a threat to the authority of the Polish party leaders as to that of the Soviet leaders.

Unfortunately, in trying to sort out the relationship of the Soviet leaders to Kania and to his successor, General Jaruzelski, one finds that little reliable evidence exists on the nature of the communications between the Soviet and Polish leaders. It is known when major Soviet leaders or the head of the Warsaw Pact forces (Marshal Victor Kulikov) made announced visits to Poland and when the Polish leaders made announced trips to the Soviet Union,[81] but it is not known what was said. It is known when the Soviet Union carried out military maneuvers in or near Poland, but it is not known when these were threats made to the Polish leaders and when they were warnings to the population designed to support the Polish leaders, maybe even at the latter's instigation. The

80. Excerpts of the text as published in Poland were reprinted in ibid., September 18, 1981. The story about the statement was carried on the preceding day.

81. U.S. Department of State, Bureau of Public Affairs, *Soviet and Soviet-proxy Involvement in Poland: Chronology, July 1980–December 1981*, Special Report 94 (GPO, 1982).

same is often true of the increasingly harsh language used in the Soviet newspapers to describe the Polish scene.

The Replacement of Kania

In response to the mounting pressure in mid-September, the Polish Council of Ministers issued a strong statement in which it charged that Solidarity was "jeopardizing the 'independent existence' of the country."[82] A few days later Prime Minister Jaruzelski told the Polish Parliament that the army would crack down on lawlessness and anti-Sovietism.[83] John Darnton of the *New York Times* was informed that the Polish Politburo had held a session extending late into the night and had seriously considered the imposition of a state of emergency, but it had followed Kania's lead in rejecting that option for the moment.[84]

Nevertheless, the fact that the Council of Ministers and its chairman were issuing such political warnings instead of the Central Committee and its first secretary was unusual in a Communist country, and on October 17 one possible explanation for this anomaly emerged. The Central Committee removed Kania as first secretary and replaced him with Jaruzelski. Kania had reportedly fallen into a state of passivity because he felt that none of the options were viable, and had been attacked by many members of the Central Committee for his lack of decisive leadership. He submitted his resignation, perhaps in the hope of receiving a vote of confidence, but 104 of the members are said to have voted in favor of accepting his resignation, 79 voted against it, and 17 abstained.[85]

The Central Committee vote probably resulted from several factors. Kania had not been a visible leader or one who had produced results, whereas Jaruzelski, a highly respected military man, might be more successful in persuading the population to abandon strikes and the activists to avoid demonstrations. In any case, a change would buy some more time from the Soviet leaders, who had been manifesting extreme displeasure. Jaruzelski, in addition to his new post as party first secretary, retained his old ones as chairman of the Council of Ministers and minister of defense—an unprecedented combination of posts in the hands of a single man in a Communist country in the postwar period.

82. *New York Times*, September 19, 1981.
83. Ibid., September 25, 1981.
84. Ibid., September 27, 1981, sec. 4.
85. *Financial Times*, October 20, 1981.

In a veiled manner the Central Committee session that elected Jaruzelski first secretary also called on the government to invoke martial law, if necessary. At the same time the government took an important step that suggested this was no idle threat: on October 17 the authorities extended by two months the term of service of members of the armed forces soon to be released. This entailed a large number of men. (Since induction into the Polish military and discharge from it essentially take place twice a year and since the term of service is two years, one-quarter of the conscripts are replaced twice a year.) Conceivably the length of the extension was simply intended to cover the period of training the new recruits, but it also suggested that the leadership expected the crisis to come to a head by December 17. At a minimum, as December 17 approached, the leadership knew that the army would revert from 125 percent of its usual size back to normal unless some other action was taken.

The Momentum Gathers

After Jaruzelski's election, the wildcat strikes continued to spread, but both the authorities and Solidarity fought to bring them under control. Their efforts met with increasing success, particularly in industry. A major strike and sit-in movement did embrace the institutions of higher education (70 of 104 institutions were to be affected by the end of November),[86] but otherwise the situation became calmer than it had been for months. Symptomatic is the fact that the *New York Times,* which since August had been averaging a front-page story on Poland every 2.5 days, carried only one between November 2 and November 27.

Beneath the surface, however, a time bomb was ticking. As noted, in September a Solidarity resolution had called for free elections, with nominations to be made by citizen groups as well as by the party. Its final program was vaguer in its call for the democratization of elections, but local elections were scheduled for February 1982 and Solidarity had to decide what to do. It either had to back down from the resolution of its congress, or it had to begin nominating candidates. Indeed, in mid-November the Silesian Solidarity called on its members to start the latter process, and dissidents associated with KOR decided to form "Clubs of

---

86. *New York Times,* November 28, 1981.

the Self-Governing Republic," presumably for the same purpose.[87] The Warsaw correspondent of the *Financial Times,* Christopher Bobinski, noted drily in late November that "the issue is of some urgency as the local government elections threaten to sweep away the Communists."[88]

In form, Poland had long been a multiparty system, with two satellite parties (the United Peasant party and the Democratic party) besides the Communists (officially known as the Polish United Workers' party). In elections the three had joined in a national front to ensure that only as many candidates were nominated in each district as would be elected, and in the same process the two minor parties were regularly allocated some of the seats in the parliament.[89] While the leaders of the minor parties may sometimes have had a modicum of influence in behind-the-scenes decisionmaking, the national front certainly seems to have corresponded closely to the Western stereotype of a Communist front that is completely dominated by the Communists.

In November 1981 the party leaders began negotiations with Solidarity, offering to broaden the front to include Solidarity and the Catholic Church. The first purpose of the front was to nominate candidates for the local elections and hence preclude independent Solidarity participations in them,[90] but the "front of national accord" of which Jaruzelski spoke would, in some ill-defined manner, also draw the participating institutions into national economic decisionmaking under the leadership of the Communist party. Solidarity scarcely felt reassured by being offered a position analogous to that of the two insignificant existing parties. It insisted on a tripartite body composed of the Communist party, Solidarity, and the Catholic Church, in which each apparently would have a veto, but its proposal was little more precise than Jaruzelski's.

On November 4 Jaruzelski met with Walesa and Archbishop Josef Glemp, the leader of the Catholic Church, and subsequent negotiations were held between the authorities and Solidarity on the question of the national front. Unfortunately, these negotiations soon broke down, and within two weeks of the November 4 meeting Archbishop Glemp had told a visitor that he believed the differences to be irreconcilable and

87. Ibid., November 16, 1981, and November 23, 1981.
88. *Financial Times,* November 27, 1981.
89. Maurice D. Simon and David M. Olson, "Evolution of a Minimal Parliament: Membership and Committee Changes in the Polish Sejm," *Legislative Studies Quarterly,* vol. 5 (May 1980), pp. 211–32.
90. *Financial Times,* November 16, 1981, and November 25, 1981.

martial law to be in prospect.[91] With Soviet leader Leonid Brezhnev scheduled to visit West Germany from November 22 to November 25 to sign an important deal on the construction of a natural gas pipeline, there was every reason to avoid confrontation before the completion of his trip. One day after his return, however, the Polish Central Committee convened and passed a decision instructing the government to ban strikes.

From this point on, events moved quickly. On December 2, the security forces were used to eject firefighter students who were conducting a sit-in at their academy. Two days later Solidarity threatened an indefinite general strike if an antistrike law were put into effect. In private discussion among the leaders Walesa termed confrontation "unavoidable," while other leaders called for the establishment of a provisional government to replace the Communist regime. The authorities in turn obtained a tape recording of this meeting and played it repeatedly on radio and television to demonstrate that Solidarity was planning to seize power. Walesa himself was called a "swindler" in the army press.[92] Conceivably a total reversal of position at this point by Solidarity could have staved off the martial law that, in retrospect, clearly was being prepared in those days, but Solidarity leaders meeting in Gdansk pushed forward. On December 12 they called for a national referendum on a provisional government and free elections. During the early morning hours of the 13th, the regime moved to arrest the Solidarity leaders and activists. At dawn, Jaruzelski announced that martial law had been declared.

The Decree and Its Effects

The provisions of the martial law decree were sweeping. Basic civil rights were suspended, and the regime was authorized to place in internment camps persons "whose behavior in the past gives rise to the justified suspicion that, if left free, they would not observe the legal order or that they would engage in activity that threatens the interest, security, or defense of the state."[93] A curfew was established for the period

91. *Los Angeles Times,* February 28, 1982.
92. *Financial Times,* December 9, 1981.
93. The documents establishing the martial law are published in FBIS, *Eastern Europe,* December 14, 1981, pp. G13–G39. Excerpts from the major decree were published in *New York Times,* December 14, 1981.

between 10:00 P.M. and 6:00 A.M., and all citizens had to carry identification cards with them. Communications were almost completely cut off. The censorship of mail was legalized, telephone service was ended, regional radio and telephone was put off the air, and most journals were closed down. Not only were private motorists forbidden to buy gasoline but travel to the border areas was prohibited. All workers' self-management organs and trade unions (the old ones as well as Solidarity) were suspended, the colleges were shut down, and strikes, demonstrations, and meetings (except for church services) were banned.

The number of people arrested at this time is unknown. Officially 5,906 were later said to have been interned, but many lesser figures were quickly released after signing a pledge to refrain from political activities. They presumably were not all included in this figure. In addition, after the original internments for pre-martial law activities, people convicted of offenses against the martial law decree were subject to formal legal proceedings and imprisonment. Their number is unknown.[94]

Martial law brought not only restrictions on the population but new political institutions as well. A Military Council of National Salvation was formed, with authority to make all key decisions. The council, which was headed by Jaruzelski, consisted of twenty-two military officials. Military plenipotentiaries were stationed in all provincial territorial subunits, and military commissars were even placed in the large industrial plants and some scholarly institutions.[95] In practice, however, the Military Council of National Salvation was too large to function effectively; an inner core of leaders informally emerged to run the country. They included Jaruzelski, his chief military deputy, the minister of the interior, Mieczyslaw Rakowski (the moderate deputy premier, who edited the weekly *Polityka* and who had handled negotiations with Solidarity), the deputy premier for economic matters, and the Central Committee secretaries for ideological questions, for organizational matters, and for internal security.[96]

From a technical point of view the imposition of martial law was

94. The claim about the original number of internees is reported in *Financial Times,* February 11, 1982. A month later it was said that a total of 486 persons had been interned for post–December 13 violations of the martial law decree, but of course the line between a martial law offense and a violation of usual criminal law in the realm of, say, vandalism, can be vague. It is not known how such violators were handled. Ibid., March 9, 1982.

95. *New York Times,* December 15, 1981.

96. *Financial Times,* February 2, 1982. In Warsaw in June I was told that the last two officials should be added to the list.

impressive. The preparations for it must have taken some time, but no one had passed effective warning to the Solidarity leaders, who were caught unaware. (Actually Solidarity leaders had received warnings of imminent arrest almost every week for a year and a half, and the warnings this time were not sufficiently different from the many false rumors of the past.) Essentially the authorities had raised the idea of troop action in a gradual way. Conducting continual polls to ascertain soldier attitudes, they had in October sent troop units into 2,000 villages to oversee the distribution of goods. By the time the troops were withdrawn four weeks later, in the second half of November, they had done little except to accustom people to the idea of troop involvement as a nonthreatening action. When the strike was broken at the firefighters academy, the regime chose an institution of the Ministry of Internal Affairs, whose students wore military-like uniforms. From all points of view, they were considered the most illegitimate of the strikers and the ones least likely to resist. Even then the troops used were not the regular army but the security forces that had been especially recruited and trained for riot control.

On December 13 and thereafter, the regime followed a dual strategy. On the one hand, it used the regular army in large numbers in the street as a visible show of force. Tanks rolled through the cities, and troops were stationed throughout in clear view. On the other hand, it used the police and security forces against actual strikes and demonstrations. Like the soldiers, members of the security forces were Poles, of course, but they were at least trained professionals rather than conscripts. They might not have consistently fired on crowds if there had been large-scale resistance, but they were not severely tested.

The extent of open resistance to martial law in the first days is difficult to judge. The authorities reported that only a few people were killed in the reestablishment of order, but one cannot be certain. The regime had every incentive to exaggerate the degree of popular acceptance, while the Western correspondents were restricted to Warsaw (which was very quiet); the radical underground sources passing on reports of unrest in the provinces also had a reason to exaggerate, but in the opposite direction from the government. When plants were closed for a considerable period of time, the explanation may have been strikes, regime fear of potential trouble, shortages of imported raw materials, or a combination of the three. In broader perspective, however, there was clearly far less resistance than many in Solidarity or the West expected.

Poland under Martial Law

As time passed, the authorities began to relax martial law in a gradual and cautious manner. For example, telephone service within the cities was restored in January 1982, then long-distance calls if made at a central telephone office, and finally home long-distance calls, although with the threat of electronic eavesdropping repeatedly announced while the phone was ringing. In early February the regime felt confident enough to reopen the universities and to raise meat prices by up to 400 percent for some popular cuts of meat. The curfew was first extended to 11:30 P.M., then lifted for three days at Easter, and in late April ended altogether. (It was temporarily restored after demonstrations on May 1 and May 3 and then made a matter of open option.) The number of internees declined to 5,067 in early January, to 4,057 in early February, and to 3,100 in early April. Another thousand were released at the end of April, but the Catholic Church reported that a substantial number were reinterned after the May demonstrations. The process of quiet release was soon resumed, and then on July 21 it was announced that an additional 1,227 would be freed. The number of original internees still under custody fell to 637.[97]

The Political Situation Today

The nature of the political situation in Poland today remains controversial. Large sections of the population have not psychologically accepted the suppression of Solidarity, and they ostentatiously show their displeasure toward those who have.[98] After a relatively quiet winter, the spring was marked by the demonstrations in early May and by strike activity on May 13. Some interpret the rise in political activity in the spring as evidence that the political situation is beginning to deteriorate again and that the probability of the Soviet Union being forced to intervene militarily may be even greater than it was before December 13 of last year. By contrast, the reporting of probably the most experienced and well-connected foreign correspondent in Warsaw, Christopher Bobinski, suggests that the situation is becoming quieter.

97. Ibid., January 11, 1982, February 11, 1982, and June 14, 1982; Stockholm Domestic Service, April 23, 1982, in FBIS, *Eastern Europe,* April 26, 1982, p. G11; and *New York Times,* July 22, 1982.

98. *Time,* June 7, 1982, p. 45.

Much will no doubt depend on events, but one should keep in mind that revolutions tend to follow certain patterns. Just as the revolutionary surge tends to continue for some time and even to become increasingly radical, so it almost always exhausts itself, at least in the medium run. People become tired. Like major earthquakes, revolutions tend to have a series of smaller aftershocks; the events of the spring of 1982 were probably these aftershocks rather than the harbinger of a new uncontrollable outburst. The fact that the curfew was lifted in Gdansk, the birthplace of Solidarity, on June 15, and in Warsaw on July 1, seems highly suggestive.[99]

At best, of course, the political situation in Poland remains complicated. By August the relaxation of martial law had reached a sensitive state, for the major remaining questions on the agenda were extremely difficult. What should be done with the internees, especially if they refuse exile? To what extent and in what ways should the leadership honor Jaruzelski's December 13 pledge of a "preservation of the basic features of socialist renewal" and a continuation of "all the reforms," including the economic reform? And did the suspension of Solidarity rather than its abolition imply that it would be permitted to function again?[100]

All the evidence suggests that the regime is determined not to permit the old Solidarity leaders and activists to play any role in any new trade union or workers' self-management organs, especially if they refuse to play a subservient role. Even before the May demonstrations, a leading Polish moderate (one might even say liberal) party spokesman, Jerzy Wiatr, told a reporter that "a few years from now, Solidarity may be reduced to a footnote in postwar history,"[101] and those demonstrations must have increased the fears of the conservatives.

The problem of what to do with the old Solidarity leadership has clearly been difficult. Given the present public mood, it has been difficult for even the moderate Solidarity leaders to facilitate their release by agreeing to play a controlled, within-system role, and Walesa himself has apparently been steadfast in his refusal to even discuss the possibility unless his advisers are present. No doubt as punishment he was not permitted to attend the christening of his child. When, however, thou-

99. Warsaw Domestic Service, June 14, 1982, in FBIS, *Eastern Europe,* June 15, 1982, p. G2; and Warsaw Domestic Service, June 24, 1982, in ibid., June 25, 1982, p. G1.
100. *New York Times,* December 14, 1981. The same theme was repeated later. See, for instance, ibid., December 17, 1982, and December 18, 1981.
101. *Los Angeles Times,* March 24, 1982.

sands of persons did attend this unannounced event, the authorities must have wondered what would happen if Walesa was permitted to function freely.

The problem of the internees has complicated the more general one of the lifting of martial law. The Solidarity leaders had been detained on the basis of the martial law decree. The lifting of martial law would mean that the internees would either have to be released or charged more formally. The authorities have, indeed, suggested that they may move against some of those who were active in building political parties before martial law (a potentially wide category, given Solidarity's support for elections), but if they were formally to try and imprison men like Walesa, they would clearly forfeit any political and economic benefits abroad that the lifting of martial law would bring them.

This is not to say, however, that nothing will change. Barring an unexpected explosion, the number of internees will surely be reduced and martial law lifted. Some type of economic reform—even including factory-level organs of workers' self-management—will surely take place. Such reform has no organic connection with political liberalization and is in fact favored by Stefan Olszowski, the conservative minister of foreign affairs. Similarly, in the agricultural sphere, laws have been passed to increase the amount of land peasants can own (earlier laws limited them to farms too small to use agricultural machinery effectively), and a real effort has been made to ensure them of the party's long-term commitment to the private sector.

The kind of Poland that will emerge in the 1980s is still difficult to define, no doubt even by the Polish leaders themselves. The tightly controlled press of the martial law period has been carrying fairly lively debates about the structure of trade unions, industrial management, and agriculture in the future. Much will depend on the relative strength of competing political forces within the Polish party and on the mood within the population. Yet progress is likely to be slow. Many Solidarity and KOR members will most likely remain interned even after martial law is lifted, and the promise of Solidarity and the spirit of renewal as it was defined in 1980–81 seems unlikely to be realized soon.

The Economic Situation Today

The future will of course depend in large part on economic developments. The country has essentially gone through a three-year economic crisis, the last year of which was particularly devastating. Even if

Western economic sanctions were removed, the enormous debt burden will limit Poland's ability to obtain credit from any prudent banker. The leaders must now try to rebuild the economy with few financial resources and with the workers sullen because of the destruction of the trade union they had created. Nevertheless, the workers' mood is not likely to improve until the economy does, and workers' self-management organs will not function effectively until they are able to make decisions about the distribution of the fruits of prosperity.

Basically Poland's economic difficulties fall into three groups. The first, much emphasized in the West, is the morale of the work force, but the problems produced by this factor have probably been somewhat exaggerated. The workers of Chile were highly politicized in the early 1970s and were staunch supporters of the radical leftist parties. Yet after General Augusto Pinochet overthrew Salvadore Allende in 1974, Chile was able to achieve an industrial growth rate of nearly 8 percent a year in the period 1976–80.[102] In Poland the basic pay system is by piece work; a worker who slows down his production only cuts his own wages or those of his brigade, or both. Someone who tries to sabotage the plant by producing low-quality goods runs the risk, first, of his products being rejected by quality control, and second, especially so long as the economy is in a recession and there is excessive labor force, of being fired. Employment levels held firm during 1980 and much of 1981, but in April 1982 the level was 5.7 percent lower than that of a year earlier.[103] One would certainly expect troublesome workers to be the first to be dismissed, and in fact managers are apparently reporting good discipline when raw materials are available.[104]

The second kind of economic difficulty in Poland involves monetary balance and relative prices. A work force, whether happy or unhappy, has little reason to perform effectively if it has no financial incentive to do so; the same is true of farmers producing for the market. So long as purchasing power far outstrips supply, extra zlotys for the worker and farmer mean little, and it is difficult to restock the stores even if production rises.

Even before martial law was imposed, the authorities had raised some prices. Afterward they carried this policy further. On February 1 they

102. Robert Solomon, "The Debt of Developing Countries: Another Look," *Brookings Papers on Economic Activity, 2: 1981*, p. 600.
103. Warsaw PAP, May 14, 1982, in FBIS, *Eastern Europe*, May 17, 1982, p. G3.
104. *Financial Times*, February 11, 1982, and May 17, 1982.

tripled the domestic price of coal, tripled or quadrupled the price of meat depending on the cut, doubled the price of agricultural machinery, and increased a number of other prices.[105] In April 1982 the overall level of food prices was 129 percent higher than a year earlier, that of alcohol products 144 percent higher, nonfood consumer goods 65 percent higher, and services 47 percent higher.[106] Since the factories can, subject to review, pass on higher costs in their finished goods prices, the higher prices of materials like coal will result in a continued increase in consumer prices for some time, especially those of manufactured goods.

The price rises of the last year have clearly been an important step toward establishing price equilibrium. Since it made little political difference in February 1982 whether the authorities doubled, tripled, or quadrupled meat prices, it would have been a monumental political error to have fallen short of what was necessary. The evidence suggests that they did not. In the summer of 1980 free market meat prices were only twice as high as the rationed state prices,[107] and even with wage increases, the new prices should fill the gap. The strongest evidence that meat prices are high enough, and perhaps even too high, is that 12 percent of the meat ration coupons are not being redeemed.[108] As for the other agricultural products, the private market and state prices are said to be about the same at present.[109] Of course, equilibrium prices vary, depending on the level of production as well as demand, but the fact that the prices of eggs have already been adjusted (to be sure, downward) indicates that there will be continued marginal changes in prices to keep them in equilibrium.[110]

Besides a possible imbalance between present wages and prices, the Polish economy also faces the problem of an overhanging money supply from the past. The greater the sum of money in the hands of the population, the greater will be their disinclination to work hard (or for

105. Ibid., January 2, 1982, and February 1, 1982.

106. Warsaw PAP, May 14, 1982, in FBIS, *Eastern Europe*, May 17, 1982, p. G3.

107. *Financial Times*, August 10, 1981. Several weeks earlier Jaruzelski had estimated that food prices would have to be increased only 110 percent to meet demand. Ibid., July 20, 1981.

108. *Trybuna Ludu*, May 25, 1982, in FBIS, *Eastern Europe*, June 8, 1982, pp. G4–G6.

109. Warsaw PAP, June 3, 1982, in ibid., June 4, 1982, p. G12.

110. *Trybuna Ludu*, May 25, 1982, in ibid., June 8, 1982, p. G7. An announcement in July of a rise in wine, coffee, and tea prices explicitly indicated an intention to maintain equilibrium prices. Warsaw Domestic Service, July 2, 1982, in ibid., July 7, 1982, pp. G9–G10.

peasants to sell their goods on the market). Clearly excessive money does remain in the system, but the key question is the psychology of the population. In Japan a high savings rate is considered one of the secrets of rapid industrial growth, and if the Polish "savings" continue to be saved instead of spent, they pose little threat to the economy.

The authorities have, in fact, taken some steps to encourage saving. They have increased the value of money in savings accounts by 20 percent and offered an additional 15 percent annual interest, conditional on the depositor not withdrawing the funds for three years.[111] If the population has faith that industrial production will increase and that inflation will be restrained, this policy may be quite effective—but this *if* is a big one. When an analogous opportunity was offered farmers (payment by a bond giving 7 percent interest and redeemable in the 1983–85 period not at face value but at the indexed price of grain at the time), few chose that option instead of cash.[112]

It is likely that the problem of excess money is most severe in the countryside. At present the regime is encouraging deliveries by paying for them with a special script that is needed to purchase tractors, fertilizer, and so forth. The long-range solution must be to provide the private farmers with the opportunity to use their funds for the capital investment the sector badly needs. This requires continual reassurance about party dedication to the private sector as well as the production or importation of the needed goods.

The third main difficulty of the Polish economy is the burden of foreign debt and the adverse balance of payments—a severe problem. The estimates of the Polish hard currency debt at the end of 1981 range widely, with the Wharton Econometrics Forecasting Associates putting it at $21.9 billion, the *Economist* at $28.7 billion, and the Polish government itself at $25.5 billion.[113] Whichever figure is correct, Poland not only does not have the funds to repay the maturing loans ($7.3 billion worth in 1982) but does not even have sufficient foreign exchange to meet current interest payments ($3.2 billion in 1982).[114] That is, simply to pay its interest bill with no repayment of principal, the Poles would

111. *Financial Times,* February 2, 1982.

112. *Zycie Warszawy,* April 17–18, 1982, p. 2, in FBIS, *Eastern Europe,* April 21, 1982, pp. G17–G18.

113. "Think of a Polish Number," *Economist,* February 13, 1982, p. 13; and Warsaw PAP, April 3, 1982, in FBIS, *Eastern Europe,* April 5, 1982, p. G3.

114. Warsaw PAP, June 19, 1982, in ibid., June 21, 1982, p. G12.

have to export $3.2 billion worth of goods more than they import. As has been noted, their total hard currency exports in 1979 were $6.7 billion; it is estimated that those this year will be some $5.0 billion.[115] Moreover, if the Polish debt is approximately $25.0 billion and if it were all refinanced at the July 15 bank rate of 17 percent (the Libor rate plus 2 percent), that would mean an interest payment of $4.25 billion a year.

On the face of it, a trade surplus of the size needed to service the debt is impossible to achieve in the foreseeable future. It is not surprising that Polish authorities have begun to talk about refinancing interest payments as well as principal nor that a Polish economist has suggested that the combined Western and Communist-bloc debt to Poland must rise to the $40 billion to $50 billion level before the economy becomes fully healthy.[116] (Today, the combined total debt is probably in the $30 billion range.)[117] Yet this is hardly a solution. If Poland were to add, say, $3 billion of unpaid interest to its total debt this year, the annual interest on this amount alone would mean an additional $500 million a year at current rates. The laws of compound interest work with devastating force, especially at current rates.

Consequently, barring a sharp decline in Western interest rates and a rapid rise in the price of Polish export items such as copper and coal and in the demand for them, some of the Polish debt and interest will almost certainly have to be written off eventually, in one form or another. In fact, Poland apparently made almost no payment of principal or interest on its 1982 debts during the first seven months of the year. (It did complete payment of its 1981 interest.) In essence, de facto default has already occurred.

The foreign exchange problem has had a severe impact on Polish recovery. Sixty percent of Polish industrial raw materials are imported,[118] much of them from the West because of the Gierek program. The importation of $2.5 billion worth of raw materials and spare parts from the West is estimated to be an absolute minimum for the normal functioning of the economy. If the Polish debt problem means that the country cannot import the needed raw materials and spare parts, many

115. *Financial Times*, May 24, 1982.
116. Warsaw PAP, April 1, 1982, in FBIS, *Eastern Europe*, April 2, 1982, p. G14.
117. The Polish government has put the Western debt at $25.5 billion and the Communist-bloc debt at 3.3 billion rubles. The dollar value of the latter is difficult to calculate. *Financial Times*, January 30, 1982.
118. Warsaw PAP, April 1, 1982, in FBIS, *Eastern Europe*, April 23, 1982, pp. G27 and G29.

factories cannot operate effectively. Indeed, imports from the capitalist countries in the first quarter of 1982 were 43.5 percent lower than they had been a year before, while imports from the socialist world were up only 10.7 percent.[119]

In actuality, the Polish economy has operated in a two-tier manner under martial law. The cut-off of communication in the first weeks after December 13, 1981, had a pervasive effect, but the extractive industries soon began to recover. In the first quarter of 1982 hard coal production was up 15 percent over the comparable period in 1981,[120] and other industries based on local materials (such as electrical energy, cement, and copper) were at the 1981 level or higher. By contrast, the industries based on imports (such as the chemical industry and light industry) were in a disastrous state. Even with the increase in the extractive industries, total industrial production in the socialist sector was down 11 percent from the depressed levels of the first quarter of 1981.[121]

Although Polish officials expected the coal production in the second quarter of 1982 to be only 8.6 percent above the second quarter of 1981,[122] the first six-month total was up 16.5 percent, indicating an acceleration of production in the quarter.[123] April industrial production as a whole was down only 7.5 percent from the previous April (in the first quarter it was down 11.0 percent), and May was down only 3.7 percent. The total second-quarter production is projected at 96 percent of the 1981 figure, and the plan was apparently exceeded.[124] With hard currency exports for the first four months being put at $1.559 billion and with no debt repayments being made, that gives ample leeway for the importation of the necessary raw materials and parts.[125] The disastrous production levels of the second half of 1981 should not be difficult to improve on.

In the long run Poland does have significant economic advantages. It is one of the few countries in Europe with large reserves of coal, copper,

119. *Zycie Warszawy,* April 19, 1982, p. 3, in ibid., April 23, 1982, pp. G27 and G29.
120. Warsaw PAP, March 31, 1982, in ibid., April 1, 1982, p. G13.
121. Warsaw PAP, May 14, 1982, in ibid., May 17, 1982, p. G13.
122. *Trybuna Ludu,* March 25, 1982, pp. 1–2 in ibid., April 6, 1982, p. G9.
123. Warsaw PAP, June 30, 1982, in ibid., July 1, 1982, p. G10.
124. *Trybuna Ludu,* March 25, 1982, pp. 1–2, in ibid., April 6, 1982, p. G9; Warsaw PAP, May 14, 1982, in ibid., May 17, 1982, p. G3; and *Trybuna Ludu,* June 17, 1982, in ibid., June 25, 1982, p. G7. The first six months' production was lower than that of the previous year by 6 percent; with the first quarter down 11 percent, that implies a second quarter almost equal to that of the previous year. Warsaw Domestic Service, July 5, 1982, in ibid., July 6, 1982, p. G5.
125. *Trybuna Ludu,* May 27, 1982, pp. 4–5, in ibid., June 11, 1982, p. G4.

and timber. As Japan has demonstrated, however, raw materials are hardly the indispensable key to economic growth, and one might even argue that they distract a country from what needs to be done. Poland surely will not realize its economic promise without substantial economic reform—consolidation of the tiny farms so that more agricultural investment is possible, a change in the industrial incentive system to reward innovation and quality, a winning of the trust of the workers, and so forth. The Polish leaders recognize this need verbally, but only the future will tell whether their words will be translated into deeds.

In the short run several factors will be crucial. One is the strength of the world market. In early spring Poland was able to sell only about 80 percent of the coal that it had available for export, and world prices were 10 to 15 percent lower than the 1981 average.[126] A Polish article reported that "our ships, laden with coal, wander from port to port in search of clients."[127] It is not clear how much of this problem is attributable to political factors, how much to the general decline in demand because of the recession, how much to an inflexible Polish pricing policy, and how much to buyers locking themselves into contracts with other suppliers when the Poles failed to meet their commitments in 1980 and 1981. The quantity of coal exported has been rising,[128] but the funds received from sales will not improve dramatically until the Western economies begin a substantial recovery. The fall of copper prices by 20 percent in the first six months of 1982 dwarfed the effect of the 4 percent increase in copper production on foreign earnings,[129] but of course a return to old price levels would have a corresponding effect in the other direction.

A second crucial factor is the success with which the Poles are able to replace Western trade links with Eastern ones. Many Polish goods and raw materials are prized in the Communist world, but the usability of imports from the East is a problem. The main consumer shortages in Poland today are of shoes and clothing; items imported from the East, such as cotton and rawhide (though not necessarily artificial fibers), are easily substitutable for Western goods. Industrial raw materials are more difficult to substitute, especially in Western-made machines that were

126. For an excellent article on the subject, see *Los Angeles Times*, April 28, 1982, part 4.

127. Warsaw Domestic Television Service, reporting on an article in *Zycie Gospodarcze*, in FBIS, *Eastern Europe*, April 1, 1982, p. G14.

128. *Financial Times*, June 2, 1982.

129. *New York Times*, January 1, 1982, and July 1, 1982; and *Trybuna Ludu*, June 28, 1982, in FBIS, *Eastern Europe*, July 2, 1982, p. G1.

built to use Western semifabricated goods. The overall scale of the substitutability of these materials and the speed with which the substitution can be done are not certain.

A third factor is the foreign currency situation. If formal default and subsequent lawsuits tie up even cash trade (say, coal shipped abroad is seized for payment of past debts), default would provide yet another shock to the economy. The likelihood of such a scenario is unclear. One would think that European suppliers of raw materials are uneasy about the loss of their Polish markets to socialist countries, that European banks are uneasy about their debts, and that therefore European governments would move to insulate current trade from default. One would also think that international institutions and even the United States would worry about precedents being established in the Polish case that might be applied later to a friendly country in similar straits.

In the short run, even without major reform, the prospects of the Polish economy are probably brighter than is generally assumed. The economy is so depressed that it would experience substantial growth simply in returning to previous levels of production. Annual hard coal production, as mentioned, declined from 200 million tons in 1979 to 163 million tons in 1981. In the summer of 1981 Polish planners estimated that even a return to a 175 million ton level (a 7.5 percent increase) would result in overall industrial growth of 5 percent, and the present prediction is for production of 185 million tons in 1982.[130] An increase in coal production will not have as big an effect on industrial production today, but one should not concentrate only on the difficulties of reaching the production levels of 1979. It will be much easier to improve conditions from the very low levels that they have reached. With the changes in price structure giving the population the sense that there is a direct relationship between their own work and their ability to purchase goods, this short-term improvement may be crucial from a political point of view.

U.S. Policy toward Poland

The eruption of Poland in the summer of 1980 caught the U.S. government at an awkward time. An election campaign was in progress

130. For an illustration of ways in which Polish planners link their projections of economic recovery directly to different assumptions about the level of coal production, see Zbigniew M. Fallenbuchl, "Poland's Economic Crisis," *Problems of Communism,* vol. 31 (March–April 1982), pp. 18–19. For the 1982 prediction, see *Financial Times,* June 2, 1982.

but, more important, the grain embargo and other sanctions placed on the Soviet Union because of the Afghanistan invasion affected relations with Eastern Europe. (For example, the outstanding CCC credits to Poland had fallen from $800 million in December 1979 to $724 million in June 1980.)[131]

The response of the Carter administration to the events in Poland was cautious. The administration extended a final $670 million in agricultural credits to try to alleviate the food shortages,[132] and it warned the Soviet Union not to intervene and the Poles not to engage in excesses. The latter point was driven home by publicity about Soviet troop maneuvers and alerts. When the AFL-CIO decided to provide Solidarity with financial aid in September 1980, Secretary of State Muskie talked with Lane Kirkland, president of the AFL-CIO, in an effort to dissuade him.[133]

When the Reagan administration came to power in January 1981, it inherited a situation that was obviously deteriorating. The first great scare of a Soviet invasion had just passed, but there was no sign of stabilization and the second invasion threat was to emerge in late March. Basically, for whatever reason, the administration followed a policy of doing little. The Reagan administration added $71 million worth of surplus dairy products to the $670 million of agricultural credits that had been granted by the Carter administration. But when the Carter credits were exhausted, the Reagan administration offered new commodity credits of only $50 million.[134] Stung by criticism that its warning about Soviet troop movements helped the Soviet war of nerves on Poland, the administration became more restrained in doing this.

There were those who believed that the inaction of the Reagan administration and its refusal to offer large-scale aid to Poland reflected a hope that the situation in Poland would continue to deteriorate and that the Soviet Union would be compelled to invade. The hope, it was charged, was that an invasion would bog down the Soviet Union and help to unite Western Europe against it. While some of the more ideological elements within the administration may indeed have entertained such thoughts, it should be recognized that the United States had few reasonable options. Given the continual rise in the excess purchasing power in Poland in 1981 and the delay in increasing prices, anything other than massive aid would have made no difference. No American

131. *Status of Active Foreign Credit,* June 30, 1980, p. 76.
132. *New York Times,* November 28, 1981.
133. Ibid., September 4, 1980.
134. Ibid., July 29, 1981.

government was in a position to offer such aid without demanding major political conditions, and the Soviet Union would never have tolerated the acceptance of such conditions, all the more so from a hard-line U.S. administration. A policy of inaction was probably the most sophisticated that the United States could have followed and may well have reflected careful calculation.

When martial law was declared on December 13, 1981, the Reagan administration again acted slowly. It took no concrete actions for ten days, and even then it limited itself to stopping Export-Import Bank credits, suspending all government-sponsored shipments of agricultural products, prohibiting Polish airline flights to the United States, and denying Polish fishermen access to American waters.[135] (It also imposed rather mild sanctions against the Soviet Union, avoiding the one significant measure that it might have taken—a reimposition of the grain embargo.)[136] Subsequently, the administration steadfastly refused to declare the Polish government in default on its debts, even though such a declaration would have been proper (and perhaps even obligatory) when the administration was forced to pay the banks on the CCC loans that it had guaranteed and that had not been repaid.[137] Only on June 18 did it try to impose meaningful restrictions on the Soviet construction of a pipeline to Western Europe.

The United States placed three major conditions on a return to normal relations with Poland: an end to martial law, the release of the prisoners who had been interned, and a renewal of the government's dialogue with Solidarity and the Catholic Church. Indeed, the administration coupled the promise to sheathe the stick with an offer of a carrot if these commitments were met. President Reagan said, "If the Polish Government will honor the commitments it has made to basic human rights in documents like the Gdansk agreement, we in America will gladly do our share to help the shattered Polish economy, just as we helped the countries of Europe after both world wars."[138]

Since few expected the Polish government to meet Reagan's conditions in full, the real question was what the administration intended to do if they were met in part. If, as in the aftermath of the Hungarian

135. Ibid., December 24, 1981.
136. For an analysis of these sanctions, see John P. Hardt and Kate S. Tomlinson, "Economic Interchange with the U.S.S.R. in the 1980s," paper prepared for Conference of California Seminar on International Security and Foreign Policy, April 1982, pp. 26–30.
137. *New York Times,* February 1, 1982.
138. Ibid., December 24, 1981.

revolution, some prisoners were retained for a decade, would it take that long for the United States to return to normal relations with Poland? Or would simply the ending of martial law provide the occasion for some relaxation of restrictions? Reasonably enough, the administration has not answered these questions in public and probably has not decided on them in private.

Present Difficulties and Choices

In the short run U.S. policy toward Poland depends on actions taken by Poland and the Soviet Union. Even if it wants to, the Reagan administration will not find it easy to remove sanctions if martial law remains in place and Solidarity leaders of the stature of Lech Walesa remain interned or, worse, are formally charged and imprisoned.

In the medium run the dilemmas that historically have faced the United States in its policy toward Poland will continue to exist. On the one hand, it is likely that the Polish authorities will be able to gradually reduce the most severe restrictions that they imposed on December 13 and that martial law itself will be lifted this year. The Soviet Union is unlikely to have to intervene militarily. On the other hand, it is almost impossible to imagine a national-level Solidarity with any real political or even economic independence being established soon. The level of political freedom will certainly not return to that which existed between September 1980 and December 1981 and will probably not return even to the level found from 1976 to 1980 under Gierek. Many radicals will undoubtedly remain in jail, and the release of others is likely to be conditional on their withdrawal from political life.

Given this probable ambiguity in Polish developments in the coming months and even years, the United States will continue to face difficult choices, none of them wholly satisfactory. If the administration takes the maximalist position and makes the removal of sanctions conditional on Poland meeting all its demands, it runs the risk of locking itself into sanctions at a time when they will become increasingly burdensome. Since the Polish repayment of foreign debts depends on its export earnings, which in turn depend on the Polish ability to obtain crucial spare parts and raw materials abroad, the Western European governments and banks will be under growing pressure to ensure that this business is not irrevocably lost to the Communist bloc. The fact that they have resisted the declaration of formal default even in the face of total nonpayment by Poland suggests that they are already feeling the pressure. They are likely to want to provide additional loans or simply to ignore the repayment question so that the Poles will have money available for purchases. Even if Poland is declared in formal default, countries like West Germany and Austria will probably want to have cash-and-carry relations with Poland. Since U.S. sanctions and denial of credit center primarily on food, they have the appearance of an attempt to worsen the Polish people's diet as a punishment for being politically repressed. They will be more difficult to defend politically once the worse features of martial law are eased and the Western European allies begin removing their sanctions.

If the United States makes the removal of sanctions or the granting of credits conditional on partial concrete reforms, it faces two additional problems. First, it runs the risk that explicit demands for reforms will be counterproductive, that the Polish government will feel itself unable to yield to open pressure just as the Soviet Union would not accept the open linkage of Jewish emigration to most-favored-nation treatment in the Jackson-Vanik Amendment in 1974. Second, in making action conditional on partial reform, the United States gives the impression that it is legitimating any forms of repression whose removal it is not demanding. This problem will be even greater if Poland follows its announced policy of exiling extremist Solidarity leaders. There will then be many people coming to the United States who will be as likely to take a maximalist position abroad as they did at home and who will charge the U.S. government, if it is at all flexible, with a betrayal of the Polish people.

As the United States decides how to respond to this situation, the most basic question is the priority of its objectives. To what extent is it seeking to promote a gradual increase in freedom and autonomy in Poland and to what extent is it simply using Poland as a pawn in its policy toward the Soviet Union? Indeed, in its relations with the Communist world in general, to what extent is the United States trying to promote the evolution and to what extent the collapse of the system?

In an ideal world the United States and its Western European allies should follow a political and economic policy that will overthrow the Soviet dictatorship in the next few years. Such a policy might cause more pain for the Polish people in the short run, but in the long run the suffering produced by an economic warfare policy would, if successful, surely be a small price to pay for freeing the Polish people from Russian control and giving them the right to choose their own form of government.

In the real world, however, politics is—or should be—the art of the possible. What are the probabilities that an economic warfare policy would be successful? While the prediction of the future of any political system is dangerous, there are grave reasons to doubt that such a policy would work.

First, political support in the West for a consistent policy of economic warfare does not exist. Although many think that the Soviet Union is now in a position to be punished, few think that the system can be overthrown in the near future, and without that conviction the many forces that oppose a policy of economic warfare will surely reduce it to a policy of nagging irritants.

The most obvious limits on a policy of economic warfare are those imposed by other countries. If Argentina and Canada would not sell grain to the Soviet Union, a grain embargo might work. If Western Europe and Japan would not sell technology to the Soviet Union or help finance and build a natural gas pipeline, the Soviet Union would be deprived of valuable foreign currency. All this is true, but it is also true that if horses could fly, they would once have made an excellent instrument of aerial surveillance.

Serious policy should not rest on dreams, but on an understanding of the realities of the world. It is a dangerous illusion that the policies of Western Europe or Japan are ours to control. In 1950, when Western Europe was much weaker than the United States, only Great Britain and Turkey would even provide significant military units to the United Nations forces in Korea.[139] Now that NATO and Japan have an industrial production and a quantity of troops greater than those of the United States, why should we expect them to act in a less sovereign manner than before? If we cannot prevent Argentina from engaging in a counterproductive war over the Falkland Islands, how can we prevent Argentina from engaging in highly profitable grain trade with the Soviet Union?

There are also, it should be noted, serious U.S. domestic restraints on an economic warfare policy. The United States has sustained a trade embargo with Cuba for twenty years, as it did with China for a longer period. Nevertheless, the political pressures on the trade of grain—the main American export—are now apparent. With the United States in a position of overproduction and the grain market soft, this situation will

139. T. R. Fehrenbach, *This Kind of War* (Macmillan, 1963), pp. 445–46. The United States contributed ten times the number of troops of all other nations combined, except for Korea.

not change soon. Even in the area of industrial trade, it is far from clear that the present support for restrictions will continue for long. If economic conditions do not improve dramatically, U.S. anger at losing business to the Europeans will grow, and it is possible that the objections will spread to restrictions in this hemisphere as well.

The long-range sanctions against Poland are on even shakier ground than those against the Soviet Union. Poland has neither nationalized American industries as Cuba did, nor has it fought the United States as China did in Korea. The notion that the Polish people should be punished economically simply because they were suppressed politically is an uncomfortable one to live with. This is all the more true when sanctions seem to harm U.S. strategic interests by making Poland more dependent on the Soviet Union. Also, the Polish-American community's pressure on the government may intensify, either because it does not want Poland used as a pawn in relations with the Soviet Union or because it feels that full contacts with relatives in Poland depend on normalizing U.S. relations with that country.

A second problem with a policy of economic warfare is that the Soviet Union is not likely to collapse in the near future. Even though it has been on the same treadmill that Poland was on—importing huge amounts of grain to produce meat that is sold well below cost and hence will always be in short supply[140]—it has a much stronger financial position than Poland had. The Soviet Union is estimated to have had a reserve of 1,844 tons of gold at the end of 1981 and a production of 328 tons a year at that time.[141] At $325 an ounce for gold, such a reserve would be worth over $19.0 billion and the annual production nearly $3.5 billion. Petroleum and natural gas exports to the West were worth $17.0 billion in 1980, and while the petroleum sales will probably be declining in the 1980s, the natural gas pipeline being built to Western Europe will produce net earnings of some $8.0 billion when it comes on line in 1986 or 1987.[142]

---

140. The Soviet Union imported 20.6 million metric tons in the 1976 crop year, 10.6 million in 1977, 22.4 million in 1978, 24.2 million in 1979, 28.3 million in 1980, and an estimated 40.0 million in 1981. If it paid some $160 a metric ton landed in the USSR, the cost since 1978 alone would have been $18 billion. U.S. Department of Agriculture, East Europe and USSR Branch, *USSR: Review of Agriculture in 1981 and Outlook for 1982* (GPO, 1982), pp. 12, 30.

141. *Financial Times,* January 15, 1982.

142. Edward A. Hewett, "Near-Term Prospects for the Soviet Natural Gas Industry, and the Implications for East-West Trade," *Soviet Economy in the 1980s: Problems and Prospects* (GPO, forthcoming).

The Soviet Union had a net hard currency debt of only $10.2 billion in 1981, and even if, as the Wharton Econometrics Forecasting Associates projects, this rises to $25.9 billion by 1985,[143] the debt service would not be an intolerable burden for a country with its scale of exports and gold production.

More fundamentally, the relationship between nationalism and communism is very different in the Soviet Union than in Poland. In Poland (and in all the Eastern European countries except Yugoslavia and Albania), communism was imposed from the outside and meant the loss of national independence. Consequently, the force of nationalism has worked heavily against stability in these countries. In Russia, as well as in Albania, China, Cuba, Vietnam, and Yugoslavia, the Communists came to power essentially on the strength of internal forces and identified themselves with the forces of nationalism both before they gained power and afterward. As a result, all these regimes have been quite stable— remarkably stable for third world countries in the twentieth century.

In Russia, in particular, communism has been closely associated with the achievement of important national goals. Russia lost the Crimean War to Britain in 1856 and the Russo-Japanese War in 1905, and its performance in World War I was abysmal. Under communism Russia gained sufficient military strength to defeat Germany in World War II and to become one of the two great superpowers in the postwar period. The multinational character of the Soviet Union has linked the Communist party with Russian nationalism in another and perhaps more important way. A strong centralized party means that Moscow controls the border republics, and a prohibition on competing parties prevents the rise of nationalist parties in those areas. Even liberal Russian intellectuals often express the fear that the establishment of Western democracy in Russia would lead not only to the loss of Eastern Europe and the advance of Western military power to Russia's European borders but also to the break-up of the Soviet Union itself as a country. It is this assumption that leads many Russians to view American support of Soviet dissidents as a cynical attempt to weaken the power of an adversary and to view the dissidents themselves as traitors who serve the United States in that effort.[144]

143. *Wharton CPE Balance of Payments and Debt Review*, July 23, 1982.

144. Of course, the same factors that strengthen the support of the Russian people for the Communist regime tend to weaken the support of the non-Russian people in the Soviet

For this reason, if demonstrations and strikes occur in the Soviet Union—which is certainly possible—they are likely to be more similar to those that have occurred in the United States in recent decades than to those in Iran or Poland. Without the threat of Soviet intervention, the turbulence in Poland would surely have swept away the political system as completely as did the demonstrations against the shah in 1978. But even the riots of the mid-1960s in the United States, let alone those in Miami more recently, never had the potential to produce a similar result. The identification of communism with Russian nationalism means that major unrest in the Soviet Union—at least the first wave of it—will probably take the latter form.

The Soviet Union of 1982 is also different from the Poland of the late 1970s precisely because Gierek's policies had the consequences described in this study. The people of the Soviet Union (and of Eastern Europe) know that the revolutionary upsurge in Poland ultimately resulted in economic hardship and renewed political repression. If there is perceived to be a chance for gradual, evolutionary improvement, the temptation for other peoples to follow the Polish path is likely to be small. The Soviet leaders have also learned many lessons from Poland. They are now aware of the danger of financial overextension, and they must realize that the policy of freezing food prices has potentially grave consequences and cannot be continued forever. They also now know—to quote Richard Kosolapov, the chief editor of the Central Committee's theoretical journal, *Kommunist*—that "socialist consciousness of workers and toilers in general [for which read "political support"] is not transmitted in genetic code to new generations" and that it must continually be relearned. This is "one of the indispensable and most difficult tasks of a Marxist-Leninist party."[145] It is widely recognized that the Soviet economy is in trouble and that something must be done.

Union for it. Yet even here there are important countervailing forces: the fear of a bloody civil war, since so many Russians live in the cities of the non-Russian republics; the ethnic divisions among the non-Russians; the pride of being part of Soviet achievements and power; the mass enrollment of educated men of each nationality into the Communist party and the consequent creation in them of a fear that they might suffer personally in an anti-Communist revolt; and, perhaps most important, a strong affirmative action program by the regime that ensures social mobility for members of the non-Russian nationalities into all significant posts within the respective republics.

145. *Pravda*, July 31, 1981. These words were printed in dark type—almost the only such ones in a long article.

Three times in the last four years, Brezhnev told the Central Committee that food shortages were a political as well as economic problem, and when he talked about the need for economic reform at the 1981 party congress and then at the 1981 session of the Central Committee, his audience applauded. Reform may not ultimately solve the Soviet problems, but for the 1980s at least it is likely to stave off political collapse.

If politics is the art of the possible—and ultimately it must be—the United States should consider far more seriously the case for an alternate line of policy that has a greater chance of success than economic warfare. The outlines of such a suggested policy will be presented in the concluding section of this study. However, Poland presents a problem that will demand decisions well before the United States has a chance to consider a basic reorientation of policy.

A Policy for the Future

If the United States rejects an economic warfare policy against Poland as part of a broader anti-Soviet strategy—either because it thinks that policy will not work or simply because it believes the policy immoral— it must recognize that the likely ambiguity in Polish developments is going to create increasing problems. The administration should be looking for any reasonable excuse to end the governmental sanctions against Poland and the Soviet Union, for otherwise they are going to become increasingly unproductive and difficult to remove. The formal lifting of martial law in Poland might be an appropriate occasion. The United States should not make normal relations with Poland dependent on major political reform but concentrate its diplomacy on issues in which it has a clearly legitimate interest by international convention— for example, relations between the members of the Polish-American community and their families in Poland.

A distinction should be made between a return to normal economic relations and the granting of aid or subsidized loans. The most graceful political way out of the present American dilemma would probably be to couple the removal of sanctions with the repetition of the promise of major aid to Poland, conditional on the acceptance of the administration's maximum demands. Although the probability of such conditions being met is low, it would not be counterproductive to make the try. If the conditions are not met, the denial of the aid could be seen as a response to the continued repression.

The most effective American support for political reform in Poland would be indirect. American diplomats could certainly point out to the Polish authorities informally that American bankers are concerned about the effect of worker morale on future economic performance and ability to pay. They could suggest to the Poles that steps which seemed to address this problem (for example, more self-management for workers) would no doubt reassure the bankers; in turn it should not be difficult for the government to suggest to the bankers that they should be reassured in these circumstances. The kind of informal discussion with the Soviet government that facilitated Jewish emigration from the Soviet Union in the late 1960s and early 1970s might be fruitful in the 1980s with Poland on a different issue—certainly more fruitful than overt demands. Polish entry into the International Monetary Fund would be beneficial; IMF conditions in the realm of prices, interest rates, and monetary policy would probably be much more acceptable than direct U.S. conditions and might even be welcomed by the Polish authorities to justify painful, but needed, price adjustments in the future.

Basically, however, it needs to be understood that the question of Polish foreign economic relations and international financial recovery is not primarily—or perhaps even significantly—one of bilateral Polish-American relations. First, the economic facts of life dictate that Western Europe rather than the United States will have the greatest influence on Poland. Since the bulk of Polish Western trade is with Europe and since the bulk of Polish loans are due to Western European governments and banks, they will have to make the main decisions on default, on terms of current trade, and on the aid that is appropriate. Western Europe should now assume more of the burdens of the relationship between the industrial democracies and the Communist world. With regard to aid, it is natural for Europe to concentrate on areas geographically close to it, while the United States concentrates on areas like the Caribbean.

Second, the Polish debt problem will almost surely have to be treated in the context of the general problem faced by countries at low or medium levels of development without major petroleum reserves. The combination of recession and high interest rates in the West has had serious consequences for almost all such countries.[146] (Symptomatic of the problem is the fact that thirteen nations are now in arrears in their

146. Solomon, "Debt of Developing Countries," p. 606. From 1977 to mid-1981 the interest rate on three-month deposits in the Eurodollar market rose from 6.00 percent to 17.75 percent. Ibid., p. 596.

interest payments to the United States for armament purchases.)[147] The recession has caused a big decline in the demand for commodities and in their prices at the same time that large export surpluses are needed to finance high interest payments. If a country falls into de facto default and must add its delinquent interest payments to the principal of its loans, the situation can quickly get out of hand. To repeat, if Poland fails to pay $3 billion interest this year and thus increases its debt by that much, the next year's interest on that $3 billion alone would be over $500 million at current rates. Unless the West soon experiences much lower interest rates and a rapid economic expansion, the international community will undoubtedly have to work out some mechanism to deal with bankrupt countries—a mechanism that involves a partial forgiveness of debt or interest. These arrangements, while primarily developed for third world countries, will be relevant for Poland as well.

Third, the main potential American contributions to the solution of the Polish problem are probably to be found in the political rather than the economic realm. This study has focused solely on the domestic Polish scene and Poland's international economic relations. But Poland is also a key element in the East-West military balance in Europe—and a tragic one at that. The Western concern about the conventional balance between the Warsaw Pact and NATO always includes the Polish divisions among the Warsaw Pact troops, but when the Soviet generals make the same calculation, they certainly do not count on Polish troops for much help. The reliance on security troops in the imposition of Polish martial law suggests that the Polish troops are also not counted on heavily to maintain Polish domestic stability.

In these circumstances one can imagine that Poland might have an important part in the conventional arms reductions in Europe that President Reagan has begun to mention.[148] If a reduction in the size of the Polish armed forces would make the West feel less threatened by the Warsaw Pact without lessening the Soviet sense of security, it seems a beneficial step to take—and one which would be of significant economic benefit to Poland as well. Such a reduction is an issue that should be explored carefully once martial law is lifted.

Finally, of course, the United States must remember that the extent to which the Polish people will be able to live a freer life will largely

147. *Washington Post,* July 12, 1982.
148. *New York Times,* June 10, 1982, and June 18, 1982.

depend on developments in the Soviet Union. If men come to power in the Soviet Union who begin to put the country on a war footing, the consequences for Polish freedom will be grim. If, on the other hand, the new Soviet leaders initiate liberalizing reforms, they will have little hesitancy about granting Poland the freedom to take similar measures. The more pluralistic the Soviet political system becomes and the less dogmatically its leaders look at the world, the more they will be able to look with equanimity at pluralism within Eastern Europe. Insofar as the United States has an influence on Polish developments, it is likely to be through its policy toward the Soviet Union and the Communist world in general.

U.S. Policy toward the Communist World

In the last decade the major competitor to a policy of economic warfare was détente, but that policy has not been well understood by the American people. Indeed, the various proponents of détente themselves had contradictory and ill-defined conceptions and defenses of it.

To a large extent, détente was described in the United States as the granting of economic concessions to the Soviet Union in exchange for political concessions by the Soviet Union in the third world. The first part of the Brezhnev era (mid-1960s to early 1970s) had featured an activist Soviet policy in the third world. The Soviet Union had provided important military aid to North Vietnam for its conquest of South Vietnam, had begun the construction of military bases in Yemen and Somalia, and had placed surface-to-air missiles in Egypt with Soviet advisers. Many people in the United States hoped that the development of strong economic relations with the Soviet Union would blunt the thrust of its drive.

For several reasons, trying to link economics to Soviet third world behavior never proved to be a successful policy. First, the Jackson-Vanik and Stevenson amendments meant that the United States never made its economic offer at all credible. Second, the third world question was a low-priority goal for the Western Europeans. Their success in meeting goals of greater importance to themselves gave them no reason to curtail their rapidly expanding economic relations with the Soviet Union. Third, the United States was never clear in its own mind about the type of Soviet restraint in the third world that was acceptable—other than an end to Soviet involvement, which the Soviet Union was not likely to believe was compatible with its Great Power status and which it certainly was not going to trade for the economic pittance being offered. When Zairian troops, backed by China and probably also by the United States, threatened to defeat the forces in Angola that were backed by the Soviet Union and the Organization of African Unity, the Soviet Union felt fully justified in supporting Cuban troops.

Détente also had a military side—and the SALT I treaty was, in fact, the chief symbol of success for that policy—but here, too, the various proponents of détente were pursuing different goals. Some saw détente as a way to continue the attack on the "military-industrial complex" that had begun during the Vietnam War, that is, to ensure that the increase in military expenditures brought about by the war would be reversed and the dividend directed to social goals. Others saw détente—and especially the SALT treaty—as a way to reassure the population about nuclear war and legitimate the expenditures of strategic weapons that they believed had been neglected during the war.[149] In practice, the SALT I treaty did essentially "limit" the Soviet and American military to the weapons programs that each wanted.

If a reasonable alternative to economic warfare is to be posited for the 1980s, its goals must be defined in a clearer and a more realizable way than they were in the 1970s. The health of the U.S. body politic has been seriously harmed by an exaggeration of threats that can then never be successfully parried and by the posing of unrealistic goals that can never conceivably be attained. The result—at a time when the internal difficulties of our much poorer adversary have been becoming steadily more severe—is an intensification of a sense of weakness that has lasted for a quarter of a century. Those who speak of a post-Vietnam malaise should not forget that the sense of weakness and threat was as strong during the Eisenhower administration in the late 1950s as it is today. That was the time of the launching of Sputnik, the missile gap, the victory of Fidel Castro in Cuba, and the perception of Gamal Abdel Nasser of Egypt as the Soviet proxy in the Arab world and Patrice Lumumba as its proxy in Africa. John F. Kennedy's campaign was geared to this malaise, and an essential part of his program was a 25 percent increase in the military budget. Two administrations became involved in Vietnam in large part because they feared the domestic consequences of simply abandoning it.

149. Henry A. Kissinger, *Years of Upheaval* (Little, Brown), pp. 133–35, 236–37.

The Three Goals of Policy

The first goal that should be at the heart of an alternative to economic warfare is the familiar one of reducing the danger of nuclear war. This study is not the place for discussing the intricacies of nuclear strategy, but this goal should not be limited to creating an atmosphere of good will. It should focus on controlling those weapon systems that have the clear capability of making a first strike on the strategic forces of the other side. Counter-force weapons and strategies have the awful consequences of giving each side the incentive to strike first if it thinks that war is imminent and that its opponent will attempt to destroy its ability to retaliate.

The second goal of policy should be to encourage economic reform, the development of a greater tolerance of diversity, and a more open attitude toward the outside world among the Russians. In 1965, as may be recalled, Brzezinski predicted that détente would encourage the liberalization of Eastern Europe and that developments in those countries would spread to the Soviet Union. In succeeding years both détente and liberalization in Eastern Europe have had an uneven history; one of the countries with which the United States has had the greatest contact—Romania—has remained one of the most repressive. Nevertheless, in general terms, Brzezinski's prediction about Eastern Europe has been accurate. Now there are signs that the prediction about the spread of the Eastern European experience to the Soviet Union will also begin coming true. For many years Soviet progressive intellectuals have been fascinated with the Hungarian experiment, but since the strikes in Poland, the authorities themselves have treated Hungary with greater respect. Brezhnev himself praised the Hungarian organization of agriculture at the 26th party congress, and the Soviet press has taken to lauding Hungarian innovations in many areas.

There are two specific reasons that Soviet economic reform is in the U.S. national interest. First, effective economic reform would require greater integration of the Soviet economy into the world economy. Many Americans assume that the basic need of the Soviet Union is to import Western technology, but the Polish experience shows conclusively that technology is no solution if the economic mechanisms do not encourage it to be used effectively.[150] What the Soviet economy really needs is for

---

150. This statement is somewhat overdrawn. A very efficient piece of machinery that does not need to be managed—for example, a turbine in a pipeline—may be very productive.

its industrialists to export technology, because only the competition of the world marketplace will provide sufficient challenge to the long-protected Soviet industry to improve the efficiency and quality of its production. The knowledge of the West and of how the Western systems really work that would come from this practical experience would be important in breaking down dogmatic Soviet views of the West.

Second, it would be difficult for the Soviet Union to introduce meaningful reform without some change in its military priorities. Market mechanisms demand rational prices, or otherwise decisionmakers will be led to irrational acts. If, for example, bread is priced below the comparable quantity of grain (as is true in the Soviet Union at present), intelligent farm managers and peasants will buy bread to feed their animals, even though such an action is counterproductive for the economy as a whole. With the Soviet economy bedeviled by many of the price imbalances previously found in Poland (not surprisingly, since Poland was closely following the Soviet model in this respect), reform will depend on many of the same politically unpopular price rises that were so explosive in that country. The most obvious way for the Soviet leaders to ease the strain of price increases on basic items is by diverting some funds from the military sphere to consumption—although of course it may not seem so obvious to them in light of other pressures and problems.

If the U.S. goal is reform in the Soviet Union and Eastern Europe rather than the overthrow of their system, it is vital that the Soviet leaders be reassured that the preconditions of reform—integration of the Soviet economy into the world economy and some limitation on military expenditures—are achievable without total surrender of the Soviet Union's position as a Great Power. It certainly can be argued that the threat of an arms race and of economic warfare was useful in reminding the Soviet leaders that they need to be more concerned about the effects of their actions on American public opinion. However, the threat needs to be coupled with assurances that the West is willing to respond to a change in Soviet behavior.

Clearly the non-American capitalist economy is large enough that Soviet economic relations with the United States are not essential to the

---

But a new factory or a new set of machines that should save on labor will surely not do so if the managers are operating under a set of incentives that discourages them from saving labor.

Soviet Union. The European resistance to American pressure for sanctions reassures the Soviet Union that access to the world market cannot be blocked; it even suggests that if the United States did not respond to Soviet reform, the Soviet Union would receive the bonus of great strains on the Western alliance. Even in the military realm, the Soviet leaders are in a position to say that the purpose of the American military buildup is to attempt to force the Soviet Union to weaken its economy by diverting resources to its military, that the Soviet Union will not fall into the administration's trap, and that the Soviet Union already has ample weapons for its announced nuclear strategy of massive retaliation.

Nevertheless, the Soviet Union remains fascinated with the United States, and it can confirm its superpower status only by dealing with the other superpower. Moreover, there are forces inside the Soviet Union that are fully capable of reacting to the American buildup with panic. Marshal Nikolai V. Ogarkov, the chief of staff of the armed forces, has gone so far as to compare the present situation with that in the mid-1930s. He has criticized the Soviet press for underestimating the danger of war and has himself called for increased preparations for possible military mobilization to meet the threat.[151] One would think that the balance of political forces inside the Soviet Union is against the Ogarkov position, but it can scarcely be intelligent for the United States to strengthen extremist views in the Soviet Union at a time of succession, especially if it serves no useful purpose.

The third goal of policy should be a gradual movement toward a depoliticization of foreign economic relations. The United States has repeatedly used economic sanctions as an instrument of policy, but they have proved singularly ineffective. Sanctions have become a political quick fix for U.S. presidents when something unpleasant occurs in the world. They create the illusion that something is being done to punish a wrongdoer, while having a low price tag in the short run.

In the long run, however, the policy of economic sanctions has been costly. In foreign policy the selective use of economic sanctions inevitably involves making relative moral judgments and hence has a political effect far beyond the specific case in which they are applied. When economic sanctions are applied against the imposition of martial law in Poland, for example, this move inevitably implies that martial law in Poland is more serious than other cases where the United States does

151. N. Ogarkov, "No strazhe mirnogo truda," *Kommunist*, no. 10 (July 1981), pp. 89–90.

not apply sanctions—for example, the imposition of martial law in South Korea or the Philippines, the Israeli occupation of the West Bank or its invasion of Lebanon, apartheid in South Africa, or the widespread military killing of civilians in El Salvador and Guatemala. Especially because of the international ramifications, this is a judgment that certainly can be defended, but Americans should not expect the defense to be convincing to those for whom the latter events have a more immediate and emotional meaning.

The domestic political costs of the economic sanctions policy—and of the posture associated with it—are as serious to the United States as the foreign ones. The fact that sanctions are sold as a meaningful way to solve a short-run political problem for an administration means that they leave the country even worse off politically when—as inevitably happens—they fail. The population becomes more convinced that the U.S. government is impotent, that its allies are betraying it, and so forth. When sanctions have to be removed before their goals are achieved (most notably in recent years in the grain embargo imposed after the Soviet invasion of Afghanistan), they intensify the sense of weakness.

The normal Soviet practice, by contrast, seems politically more astute. The Soviet Union maintained correct political and normal economic relations with the shah of Iran (even though he was a U.S. ally on the Soviet border who was buying large quantities of arms) and with the Khomeini regime (even though it is violently anti-Marxist and has executed many leftists). It is difficult to see that the Soviet Union has lost from this policy and easy to argue that it gains strongly from the policy in its long-term relations with Iran. The Soviet Union also does not seem to have lost by overlooking the deplorable human rights record of the Argentinian military regime and by developing trade relations with it.

The advantages of such a policy are greater for the United States than for the Soviet Union because of its large and wealthy private sector. Even if the U.S. government does not apply sanctions, the actions of foreign governments will inevitably affect the private decisions of American banks and multinational firms, and basically in the direction that the U.S. government desires. If, however, "sanctions" are the result of diverse private actions, then political responsibility will be diffuse and ill-defined. Indeed, when the United States does intervene for political reasons, it usually will be providing positive inducements or guarantees to businessmen to act where the risks are high, and such intervention is politically much more acceptable to the recipient and its denial much less offensive.

The Need for Self-Confidence

The U.S. government clearly needs a posture of self-confidence, and it is a posture that is fully justified. Poland is only the latest example demonstrating that the economic model developed by Stalin and adopted by the Soviet Union is a failure in the long run. The crisis in Poland is only the latest piece of evidence that Communist regimes abroad do not become automatic Soviet allies and, consequently, that the Soviet promotion of revolution is not necessarily in the Soviet national self-interest. The crisis also reminds the United States once more of the weakness of the Warsaw Pact as an offensive military alliance. Polish divisions cannot simply be added to Soviet divisions to demonstrate the scale of the Soviet threat as is habitually done; rather, the United States needs to ask how much Poland subtracts from the threat, how many divisions the Soviet General Staff has to keep in reserve for possible intervention in Poland and other Eastern European countries.

The reason for self-confidence is not less in the third world. Communist revolutions have not been occurring in the major countries that are on the road to industrialization. In fact, in countries like Brazil, Egypt, and Mexico, there are neither significant Communist parties nor the prospect for them. Instead, radical revolutions are occurring in the most backward of third world countries: Afghanistan, Angola, Ethiopia, and Nicaragua. But even there the Soviet Union is not in a position to support many Cubas economically, as it has made clear to Ethiopia, Angola, and apparently also Nicaragua.

As nearly all the leading Soviet scholars acknowledge in print, this means the third world countries will require Western foreign investment, and, as some of the most prominent Soviet scholars recognize, this will eventually mean some political dependence as well. The trend of policy both in Angola and Ethiopia illustrates the cost to the Soviet Union of being a second-rate economic power and the potentialities that the United States and its allies have in this respect.

The United States needs to adopt the posture of a Great Power, standing above trifles and promoting the well-being of its own citizens. It needs to assert confidently that the economic cards are in its hands and those of its allies, that it will not panic when some third world country—often an insignificant one in economic and political terms—undergoes a radical revolution. The United States can handle the ideological threat by the superiority of its institutions and resources, and it can handle the military threat of such a revolution by military and diplomatic means. On this latter question, one can often imagine Soviet cooperation if the situation is handled skillfully.

The United States should not simply move away from the policy of economic sanctions with a whimper. Rather, it should be forthright in declaring that a major goal of foreign policy is to promote the economic well-being of the American people, and it should embrace mutually beneficial economic relations in that framework. Indeed, by making economic well-being an announced goal of foreign policy, the United States would be laying down a challenge to the Soviet Union in an area where its system has not worked well, and would be doing so at a time when the Soviet people's irritation at its economic performance is growing. The United States could provide a goal for arms control—the mutual saving of money—that has been almost totally ignored, and do so at a time when the Soviet achievement of military equality creates the first real opportunity for a reversal of the trend of Soviet military spending. By raising the question whether the superpowers are sacrificing too much in economic growth not only by military spending but also by the direct and indirect subsidies they use to obtain and keep allies, the United States might even stimulate thought about the costs and benefits of the type of foreign political support that looms so large in superpower thinking and that often is economically extravagant. Nothing would be more conducive for greater Eastern European independence than a better Soviet recognition of the cost of empire.[152]

In recent months the Reagan administration has shown increasing awareness of the importance of the Soviet succession. At a time of monumental choices in the Soviet Union, prospective Soviet leaders need to have the vision of a possible path by which they can make the gradual transition to a better world. The president was wise to specifically offer a hand of friendship to a new Soviet leadership in his speech proposing START negotiations. Yet the world that the president seeks

152. For a discussion of the Soviet indirect subsidies to Eastern Europe, see Edward A. Hewett, "Soviet Energy: Supply vs. Demand," *Problems of Communism,* vol. 29 (January–February 1980), pp. 58–59. See also Michael Marrese and Jan Vanous, *Implicit Subsidies and Non-Market Benefits in Soviet Trade with Eastern Europe* (University of California [Berkeley], Institute of International Studies, forthcoming).

THE LIBRARY
ST. MARY'S COLLEGE OF MARYLAND
ST. MARY'S CITY, MARYLAND   20686

will demand less ideological stridency and more Great Power self-confidence than is manifested today on either side. The change in leadership that is imminent in the Soviet Union may well provide the opportunity for movement in this direction. And the United States, too, will need the inner strength to accept a world that is different from our old preconceptions. Only in such a world will countries like Poland have a real chance to gain greater freedom.